EAST
DOOR

CEDAR
ROOM

RY

ISS
FRELL's
OOM

EAST
QUANTOXHEAD
DRESSING R'M
N°. 2

KING
CHARLES'
DRESS R'M

EXPLORING BRITAIN'S
HISTORIC HOUSES

AA

Editor
Donna Wood

Designer
Andrew Milne

Picture Researcher
Liz Stacey

Image retouching and internal repro
Jackie Street

Cartography provided by the Mapping Services Department of AA Publishing

Contains Ordnance Survey data © Crown copyright and database right 2011

Production
Lorraine Taylor

Produced by AA Publishing

© Copyright AA Media Limited 2011

ISBN: 978-0-7495-6861-0
and 978-0-7495-6803-0 (SS)

Published by AA Publishing (a trading name of AA Media Limited, whose registered office is Fanum House, Basing View, Basingstoke RG21 4EA; registered number 06112600).

A04517

The contents of this book are believed correct at the time of printing. Nevertheless, the publishers cannot be held responsible for any errors or omissions or for changes in the details given in this book or for the consequences of any reliance on the information provided by the same. This does not affect your statutory rights.

Printed in Dubai by Oriental Press

theAA.com/shop

OPENING TIMES

We have given a general guide to opening times within this book, but please be aware that many of the houses, especially those that are privately owned and run, reserve the right to change their opening times without warning. We therefore strongly advise that you telephone and/or consult the website of the premises before travelling.

Right: Treasures from Versailles enhance the Regency opulence of the Drawing Room at Scone Palace

EXPLORING BRITAIN'S
HISTORIC
HOUSES

LOCATOR MAP

SCOTLAND &
THE BORDERS

NORTHERN
ENGLAND

CENTRAL ENGLAND,
EAST ANGLIA, WALES
& THE MARCHES

SOUTH &
SOUTH EAST
ENGLAND

SOUTH WEST
ENGLAND

CONTENTS

INTRODUCTION
page 6

SOUTH WEST ENGLAND | 1
page 10

SOUTH & SOUTH EAST ENGLAND | 2
page 48

CENTRAL ENGLAND, EAST ANGLIA, WALES & THE MARCHES | 3
page 96

NORTHERN ENGLAND | 4
page 146

SCOTLAND & THE BORDERS | 5
page 192

INDEX & ACKNOWLEDGEMENTS
page 222

INTRODUCTION

Ever since the first stately home threw its ornamental gates open to the public, we have been fascinated with the way the other half – or, more realistically, the other one percent – lives. But to view only the most splendid mansions is to miss out on one of the most interesting aspects of all, for each and every one of our historic houses – large or small – portrays a social and political history of Britain that no history lesson or learned volume could ever convey.

Many historic houses provide a journey through time in themselves, beginning as far back as Norman times, perhaps still occupied today by the same family and with every stage of the intervening years apparent in the fabric and contents of the house. Others appear as if frozen in time, encapsulating one particular era – a perfectly preserved medieval manor, perhaps, or the great Gothic mansion of a Victorian industrialist – a statement in bricks and mortar of new-found wealth and success and the perfect place to display artworks and treasures.

One frequently overheard comment during tours of historic houses is, '... all this for just one family!' In a way this is true, but it is not something that can be judged by today's standards. These great houses are a relic of a past way of life, and though the descendants of their builders obviously have deep affection for their ancestral homes and feel a duty to maintain them, many present-day owners readily admit to the burdens their heritage has placed upon them.

No-one would consider building on that scale today, but while ostentation certainly played its part in shaping the architectural fashions of the ages, there were practical considerations too.

Not only were families generally much larger, but they would often have a small army of staff to cater for their every need, without the benefits of electrical equipment, easy-care fabrics and convenience food, for example, that we tend to take for granted today. Every lump of coal and pitcher of hot water had to be carried from below stairs to each distant corner of the house, bath water had to be carried back down again and all those acres of carpets had to be cleaned by sprinkling damp tea leaves or pieces of paper over them, then brushing it all up again. (In Victorian times the 4th Marquess of Bath at Longleat even had a man to iron his bootlaces!). The larger of our stately homes could easily have had as many as 50 indoor staff and 30 gardeners.

Entertaining was carried out on a lavish scale, with gargantuan meals emerging course by course from the cavernous kitchens. Nor did friends and family just come for dinner – in the days when horses and carriages were the only means of transport they came to stay, sometimes for weeks or months on end, bringing their own retinue of personal servants, all of whom had to be accommodated.

Throughout history these mansions have been at the centre of great estates which were largely self-contained communities, sometimes with their own village for estate workers. What we see today as ornamental parkland would once have been a hunting ground, not simply for

Below: The housekeeper's room at Stansted Park, West Sussex, provides a fascinating glimpse of life 'below stairs'
Right: Blue and purple hues in the beautiful walled garden at Hartland Abbey, Devon

sport, but for essential food supplies. There would have been at least one farm, as well as forestry or woodland crafts, a mill, and essential services such as a forge, brew-house, joinery and dairy.

In medieval times, the lord of the manor and his family lived in close proximity to his servants and estate workers. They would all congregate in the huge Great Hall, where all the cooking, eating, entertainment and general living took place. Later came a desire for more privacy and, though life in the Great Hall went on much the same, apartments were added, into which the lord and his family could withdraw when they wished to escape from the noise and bustle.

In Tudor times great fortunes were made, and the most prominent and powerful families began to gain more of a sense of their own importance. They needed homes to suit their status – and if you were high-ranking enough to warrant a royal visit, the monarch would expect proper state apartments, reserved for their use alone, as well as accommodation for their enormous retinue of courtiers and servants. While many members of the aristocracy needed the patronage of the monarch to maintain their position – or simply to keep their heads in some instances – most would dread the disruption and crippling costs of a royal visit.

It was during this time that Henry VIII broke with Rome and declared himself head of the church in order to obtain a divorce. Monastic foundations, such as Forde Abbey, were dissolved and many of these came into private hands to be converted for family living, adding another dimension to our architectural heritage.

Fortunes could change overnight in those days. A change of king – or a king who changed his mind – could make or break a family, and their homes reflected the circumstances which arose. This was no more so than during the English Civil War (1642–49), when houses designed for peaceful living found themselves besieged and battered. Some escaped war damage only to be sacked by the victorious Parliamentarian forces in retribution for Royalist sympathies.

The geographical location of the house also contributed to the way in which it was built and inhabited. For many centuries no important house was built in the border country between England and Scotland without being properly fortified, as this was an area of disputed territory, with the border moving back and forth with each minor victory, and frequent cross-border raids. Great pele towers were built, which were easy to defend and large enough for the surrounding cottagers to take refuge in times of trouble. Many of the grand houses of Cumbria and Northumberland still have a pele tower at their core. Within Scotland similar struggles over land and property were taking place between the clans, and visits by neighbours frequently heralded not inconsiderable bloodshed. Many of the great mansions along the Welsh border began as castles – outposts of the Norman conquerors, where loyal knights stood at arms against any insurgence from the Welsh princes. When times became more peaceful within the country, the aristocracy broadened their horizons, and this had an enormous impact on the style of the country house. Young men were dispatched on Grand Tours of Europe in order to improve their minds and their appreciation of the arts. Many returned with huge collections of antiquities and paintings, often with absolutely no thought as to where they would all be put. Houses were extended or rebuilt, and the fashion was to display these treasures in suitably classical surroundings. Tudor and Jacobean facades were swept away in favour of great columned porticoes and sweeping staircases, warm wood-panelled interiors were transformed with marble pillars, intricately decorated plaster ceilings and classical friezes, and special galleries were created to house statues and marbles. Remembered now as a stern and highly moralistic people, the Victorians nevertheless produced some flamboyant and hugely entertaining architecture. Having no taste for the immediate past, and little interest in conservation and heritage, they harked back to a distant age of chivalry, creating fairy-tale Gothic mansions weighted down with pinnacles and heraldic devices, heavy and intricately carved wood panelling and enormously sturdy furniture. The term 'understated' could never have been coined during the 19th century!

Ancient houses that had developed and changed over the centuries were suddenly catapaulted back to their original style, but with added comfort and convenience. Lacock Abbey in Wiltshire is one example of a house where original monastic features can be seen alongside Gothic Revival additions. As well as re-shaping existing buildings, the Victorians built some vast and ambitious new homes, as at Penrhyn in North Wales, looking for all the world like genuine Norman castles. This was also the time of the British Empire, when not only vast sums of money were amassed by the ruling classes, but fascinating collections of exotic items found their way into their homes, such as trophies of big game-hunting expeditions and intricately carved ivory – neither of which would be considered suitable acquisitions these days. New technology was also beginning to be applied to domestic affairs, with such luxuries as gas lighting and hot-water systems.

The Edwardian era brought both the heyday of country house society and its demise. Within a short space of time, happy and carefree house parties and great intellectual gatherings gave way to the fraught times of World War I and a permanent change in the order of our society. After the Great Depression of the 1930s and another world war, the nation's workers were far less keen to go 'into service', and by this time many of the owners of our historic houses were also struggling to survive the onslaught of death duties and other taxation.

It was around this time that houses began opening to the public as a serious business venture, a move that was frowned upon by the diehard aristocracy at the time, but one which many who opposed it at first have copied during the intervening decades. Although opening their doors to the public began simply as a means of raising much-needed revenue, most owners will readily admit that they enjoy sharing their homes and their heritage with appreciative and interested visitors.

Today there are so many historic houses open to the public that an enormous volume would be needed to include them all. This book includes a selection which, we feel, covers the whole spectrum from spectacular palaces to delightful little manor houses, from elegant country homes to the romantic turreted castles of Scotland. Every age is covered here from medieval to Edwardian, but this is not just a story of bricks and mortar (nor even of stone and oak timbers), for colourful characters and important historical figures also populate the pages of the book. We hope you will enjoy reading about them as well as visiting their fine old houses.

Left: A close-up of the balustrade on the magnificent oak staircase installed by Colonel Francis Luttrell in the 1680s at Dunster Castle, Somerset

Right: The terraced gardens of Osborne House, Isle of Wight

1	**Athelhampton** Dorset	12
2	**Berkeley Castle** Gloucestershire	13
3	**The Bishop's Palace** Somerset	14
4	**Cadhay** Devon	16
5	**Chavenage House** Gloucestershire	17
6	**Clevedon Court** Somerset	18
7	**Corsham Court** Wiltshire	19
8	**Cotehele** Cornwall	20
9	**Dunster Castle** Somerset	22
10	**Dyrham Park** Gloucestershire	23

11	**Forde Abbey** Somerset	24
12	**Fursdon** Devon	25
13	**Hartland Abbey** Devon	26
14	**Knightshayes Court** Devon	27
15	**Lacock Abbey** Wiltshire	28
16	**Lanhydrock** Cornwall	29
17	**Longleat** Wiltshire	30
18	**Montacute House** Somerset	31
19	**Newhouse** Wiltshire	32
20	**Pencarrow House** Cornwall	33

21	**Powderham Castle** Devon	34
22	**Prideaux Place** Cornwall	36
23	**St Michael's Mount** Cornwall	37
24	**Sand** Devon	38
25	**Sherborne Castle** Dorset	39
26	**Stanway House** Gloucestershire	40
27	**Sudeley Castle** Gloucestershire	42
28	**Ugbrooke Park** Devon	43
29	**Whittington Court** Gloucestershire	44
30	**Wilton House** Wiltshire	45

If any house in Britain rests cocooned in idyllic tranquillity it is Athelhampton, near Dorchester, nestled among its extensive Dorset gardens. Elsewhere in the south west, there is Powderham Castle, with its venerable tortoise and lofty grandeur; Longleat is palatial with its lions; the single and double cube rooms at Wilton are two of the most beautiful rooms in the country; and Bowood stands in one of England's most entrancing man-made landscapes. At Berkeley Castle in Gloucestershire, the Berkeley family has spent 800 years turning the brutal Norman fortress where Edward II was horribly murdered into a civilized residence. Sudeley Castle, near Cheltenham, contrives to be both a home and a romantic ruin.

ATHELHAMPTON Dorset

5 miles (8km) north east of Dorchester | Open selected days March to November | Tel: 01305 848363 | www.athelhampton.co.uk

Athelhampton's roots are in Saxon times, dating from the period when Athelhelm was Earl of Wessex, but the present building was begun in 1485.

The novelist Thomas Hardy made 'Athelhall' the setting for two rather gloomy poems and inscribed his signature into the lead of the dovecote roof. In 1891 Alfred Cart de Lafontaine built four courts walled with Ham Hill stone, as well as two garden pavilions. Yew trees were planted in the Great Court, which have since evolved into topiary pyramids. The gardens as they stand today owe much to the enthusiasm of Sir Robert Cooke, the politician, and his family, who continue his work. They restored the house following a fire in 1992, which gutted much of the east wing.

The glory of Athelhampton is its Great Hall, with a medieval roof of curved, braced timbers and an oriel with fine heraldic glass. For 500 years this has been the heart of the old house: Sir William Martyn, Lord Mayor of London in 1492, would have warmed himself here by the huge fireplace... Athelhampton, it is often said, has its fair share of ghosts!

There is much more to be seen along the winding passages and unexpected flights of stairs that link the different levels of this gloriously meandering house. The wine cellar has ancient liquor stains etched into its flagstone floor, the other rooms are festooned with panelling and tapestries, pictures, furniture and china accumulated over the centuries.

Outside the house are complex and intriguing gardens with topiary and shady walks that, like the house itself, continue to mature and grow with the passing years.

Neatly kept lawns and gravel pathways surround the medieval manor house at Athelhampton

Few families can trace their ancestry back to the Anglo-Saxons, but the Berkeleys of Berkeley Castle are in direct descent. For 1000 years the gaunt profile of Berkeley Castle has kept watch over the Severn and the Welsh borders, seeming to grow from the outcrop of rock on which it stands. Inside its thick walls, events of great importance have taken place: the West Country barons met in the Great Hall of the castle before placing their demands before King John at Runnymede in 1215; in 1327 the unfortunate Edward II was first imprisoned and then murdered in a room in the keep; during the Civil War Berkeley Castle was besieged for three days by Parliamentary forces.

Berkeley Castle was founded after Henry II granted a Charter to Robert Fitzharding in 1153, and the entry to the Shell Keep is still through a Norman doorway in the inner courtyard. Most of the building that we see today dates from the 14th century.

Berkeley Castle's Great Hall still looks much as it did when it was the meeting place of West Country barons

From the castle the views over the gardens to the river are superb. The terraces have grass walks with borders of low plants, backed by shrubs and climbers, while the bowling alley is flanked by a high wall and ancient clipped yews. Beyond, cattle graze in the water meadows, creating as peaceful a scene as anywhere in the country.

THE BISHOP'S PALACE

Somerset

In the centre of Wells | Open daily February to end of October, except for selected Saturday afternoons | Tel: 01749 988111 | www.bishopspalacewells.co.uk

Bishops' palaces are not often open to the public, and this one at Wells, behind its stout 14th-century walls and protective moat, certainly seems built to keep unwanted callers at bay. A softer impression is given by the bell above the moat near the drawbridge, which the swans come and ring with their beaks when they want to be fed.

Inside its warlike battlements the Palace has the peaceful air of centuries of clerical benevolence, its buildings set sweetly round a spacious lawn. There's a 13th-century chapel, still in daily use, and a beautiful ruined hall of the same period, which was deliberately made more picturesque in the 19th century. Both were built in the time of Bishop Burnell. What is regarded here as the 'modern' north wing was built in the 15th century by the formidable Bishop Beckynton, who was also responsible for the 'Bishop's Eye' gate, which leads to the market place.

The state rooms in the palace were transformed in 'Italian Gothic' in Victorian times, and subsequently abandoned by the bishops, who retreated to the north wing in the 1950s. A fine collection of portraits of past incumbents of the See includes the three most famous – Wolsey, Laud and Ken. The Long Gallery houses the cope that the Bishops of Bath and Wells wear at coronations, sharing with the Bishops of Durham the centuries-old privilege of supporting the sovereign.

The delightful gardens were landscaped by Bishop Law early in the 19th century, and contain the wells that give the city its name, the springs bubbling up at a rate of 40 gallons (182 litres) a second. If you are particularly blessed, you will hear the choir singing seraphically in the beautiful cathedral nearby.

Below: The Long Gallery is hung with portraits and houses the cape worn by the Bishops of Bath and Wells

Right: A peaceful air presides over the grounds

CADHAY Devon

The entrance to Cadhay is Georgian, giving little indication of the classic Tudor manor that lies within, and this is just one of the alterations carried out over many centuries to conform with the vagaries of fashion. When Cadhay's first owner, John Haydon, died he left the property to his great nephew, Robert, who had risen up the social ladder by marrying Joan Poulett, the daughter of the Privy Councillor to Queen Elizabeth I. The new squire's wife, used to the finest houses in the land, set about refurbishing Cadhay, adding on a Long Gallery in which they and their guests could perambulate in style. Having scaled the social heights, the Haydon family fell into decline, supporting the wrong side in the Civil War and then amassing debts that by 1693 exceeded £17,000.

By 1737 Cadhay was owned by William Peere Williams of Grays Inn, and the house was again remodelled. Cadhay then passed through marriage to a somewhat doubtful naval hero, Admiral Graves, who contributed to England's loss of North America through failing to relieve Lord Cornwallis.

After the death of the admiral, Cadhay began an ignominious decline. Throughout the 19th century it was let out and divided up, with farmhands crowded in its bedrooms and pigsties built against the walls. Not until 1909 did the property acquire a saviour in Mr Dampier Whetham, a Cambridge academic who rescued the house and restored it.

The architecture of Cadhay reflects the passing of time and its changing fortunes, but it remains essentially a Tudor house. Its finest feature is the internal courtyard with walls faced with stone and flint, in a random, chequerboard design. Despite the aspirations of its early owners, Cadhay remains a charmingly provincial manor house.

Cadhay's mellow Georgian entrance gives little hint of the varied architectural features to be found within

CHAVENAGE HOUSE Gloucestershire

3 miles (5km) north west of Tetbury | Open selected afternoons April to end of October | Tel: 01666 502329 | www.chavenage.com

Only a short distance from Tetbury, in rolling Gloucestershire countryside, stands the mellow stone house of Chavenage. With a central porch and two projecting bays, it is a typical Elizabethan E-shaped house.

After the Norman Conquest, Augustinian monks from Tours settled at Horsley, and the estate was administered by the Church until Henry VIII's Dissolution of the Monasteries.

Approaching the porch, it is clear that, in converting the medieval hall (whose roof would originally have been open to the rafters), much of the original fabric has been reused, including the large stone in front of the door, which might have been an altar from Horsley Priory. The main door also has a sanctuary ring and a spy hole, which again probably came from the priory. With its tall windows containing late-medieval glass, and a fine 16th-century screen with a minstrels' gallery above, the main hall still retains the authentic atmosphere of Elizabeth's reign.

During the Civil War, Chavenage played an important role on the national stage. Oliver Cromwell is known to have lodged here.

Queen Anne visited Tetbury and is thought to have lodged at Chavenage. The splendid bed that stands in her room is thought to have been converted for the use of her personal physician, and it has a Judgement of Solomon in bas relief on the headboard.

At the bottom of the stairs is a memorial chest dating from the beginning of the 17th century, while the ballroom has fine court cupboards and Cromwellian chairs upholstered in leather. The present chapel is from the early years of the last century, but contains a lovely Elizabethan monument and an important Saxon font.

The bedrooms at Chavenage housed some important guests, a fact which is reflected in their furnishings

CLEVEDON COURT Somerset

1½ miles (2.5km) east of Clevedon | Open April to end of September on selected days | Tel: 01275 872257 | **www.nationaltrust.org.uk**

This is a remarkably complete 14th-century house, and one of the oldest of its type to survive anywhere in Britain. Incorporated into it is an even older tower, built as a defence against marauding Welsh from across the Bristol Channel. Later additions and modifications have only added to the charm of Clevedon Court, without detracting from the fact that it is still considered to be typical of the medieval period.

The focal point of the medieval manor house was the Great Hall, which was divided by a screen passage. On one side was the buttery and kitchen, on the other the main body of the hall, used as the general living area of the house. Beyond were the living quarters of the lord of the manor and his family. Clevedon Court retains its early 14th-century chapel, situated on the first floor, which has beautiful and intricate tracery.

In the 18th and 19th centuries Clevedon was a meeting place for the avant-garde of the day. One owner during the late Victorian era was Sir Edmund Elton, a celebrated potter, and some of his work – Eltonware – is on display in the old kitchen of the house.

Below and right: The Great Hall is hung with portraits of the Elton family, including ten baronets

CORSHAM COURT Wiltshire

Corsham Court was built in 1582 on the site of a medieval royal manor that had, for centuries, been part of the dower of the queens of England. It was bought, in 1745, by Paul Methuen, a wealthy clothier who inherited his art collection from a relative – a distinguished diplomat who acquired Old Masters in the course of a long and widely travelled life. 'Capability' Brown's designs were employed in the house as well as the grounds, and further changes were made by John Nash. However, the character of the house as we see it today dates principally from the middle of the 19th century, when Frederick Methuen, Lord in Waiting to Queen Victoria, married Anna Sanford, a young heiress who brought with her another collection of Old Masters, many of outstanding importance. The 4th Lord Methuen studied painting under Sickert and, as a soldier in liberated France, served as Montgomery's advisor on the preservation of monuments and art.

The state rooms are splendid for their architecture and their furnishings as much as for the paintings they contain. The Picture Gallery, designed by Brown, is a triple cube, 72 feet (22m) in length, with an intricately

Corsham Court's grand architecture makes a splendid backdrop for its significant art collection

plastered ceiling and walls of crimson silk that match the furniture by Chippendale. Van Dyck's superb *Betrayal of Christ* is here, together with Rubens's *Wolf Hunt* and works of the Italian School. In the dining room are two Reynolds portraits of the children of Paul Methuen. Among other delights is an exquisite *Annunciation* from the studio of Filippo Lippi, a haunting portrait of the ageing Queen Elizabeth I and a sculpture of a sleeping cherub by Michaelangelo.

COTEHELE Cornwall

In the late 18th century Cotehele was already being shown to parties of visitors as a house of antiquarian interest. These visits were instigated by Richard, 2nd Baron Edgcumbe, whose ancestor had built the fortified manor house about 300 years earlier. Although the family had decamped to Mount Edgcumbe by the end of the 17th century, they maintained an abiding interest in their former home and a true appreciation of its historic value. Even the improvements carried out in 1862 for the widow of the 3rd Earl were implemented with a foresight and sensitivity that was rare in Victorian times.

Tucked away at the heart of its huge estate in the Tamar Valley, the house retains much of its medieval plan and a great deal of its medieval atmosphere: there is the Great Hall, hung with arms and armour beneath a high, arched timber roof; the rooms of the original solar block, with fine old furniture and tapestries on the walls; the three internal courtyards; and the fine old kitchen. The tower was added in 1620 and houses three splendid bedrooms including the King Charles' Room, where Charles I is said to have spent a night in the vast four-poster bed. Outside, wander around the formally planted terraces and explore the fascinating medieval stewpond and dovecote. At Cotehele Quay you will find the restored Tamar sailing barge, *Shamrock*. The on-site Discovery Centre tells the story of the Tamar.

The east front (above) and the Great Hall (right), hung with flags dating from the Napoleonic Wars

DUNSTER CASTLE Somerset

Set in an extremely picturesque location between Exmoor and the sea, Dunster Castle has every outward appearance of an ancient stronghold, with its great towers, turrets and battlements – but in fact these castellations were added in the late 19th century.

The castle was built in 1617 and its original fortifications were destroyed after the Civil War, by order of Oliver Cromwell. Thereafter it continued as a fine mansion and many of its handsome features, including intricately decorated ceilings and a superb 17th-century oak staircase, date from the 1680s when a great deal of restoration work was carried out by Colonel Francis Luttrell.

When it was given to the National Trust in 1976, the property had been in the hands of the Luttrell family since Elizabeth, Lady Luttrell, bought the Norman castle over 600 years ago. Nothing but the 13th-century gatehouse remains of this original building, but the Luttrell history can be traced on a tour of the castle through fine family portraits, a framed genealogy (not entirely accurate) and a display case of items which belonged to the family.

The dining room and stairhall are particularly grand, and although the morning room may lack their style and elegance, it does have wonderful views. The gallery is especially interesting for its leather wall hangings depicting the turbulent love story of Antony and Cleopatra.

Dunster Castle enjoys an unusually favourable climate and many sub-tropical plants thrive among its beautiful garden terraces, notably a huge lemon tree which bears fruit annually.

Above: The oak staircase installed by Colonel Francis Luttrell in the 1680s. The balustrade, carved from elm, sits between newel posts topped by carved vases

Left: The servants' bells, with room names above, in the corridor at Dunster Castle

DYRHAM PARK Gloucestershire

There was once a Tudor house on this site, but the Dyrham Park we see today, built for William Blathwayt (Secretary at War during the reign of William III), is entirely a creation of the William and Mary period. Blathwayt rose from fairly modest beginnings through the Civil Service to hold a number of top government jobs and found favour with William III both for his administrative abilities and because he spoke Dutch.

Blathwayt also made an advantageous marriage to the heiress of the Dyrham estate, but it was not until after the death of his in-laws and his wife that he began to build the family home.

The baroque mansion, set in a valley and surrounded by 272 acres (110ha) of garden and rolling parkland, was constructed in two stages, first in 1692 by Huguenot architect Samuel Hauduroy, and then around the turn of the century by one of the foremost architects of the day, William Talman, the architect of Chatsworth. Between them they created a splendid house that displays unusual restraint for the times. The Blathwayt family lived here until 1956, when the house was acquired by the government. In 1961 it moved into the care of the National Trust.

Dyrham Park has changed little over the years and all the furniture, paintings and pottery we see in the house today were collected by Blathwayt himself. The series of apartments display obvious Dutch influence, including paintings of the Dutch School and a collection of blue-and-white Delftware. There are Dutch-style gardens, too.

A sweeping vista from the statue of Neptune to the magnificent east front of Dyrham Park

FORDE ABBEY Somerset

4 miles (6km) east of Chard | Open selected afternoons end of March to end of October | Tel: 01460 220231 | **www.fordeabbey.co.uk**

Formally opened in 2005, the fountain at Forde Abbey is the highest powered fountain in England

From the bridge over the River Axe, close to the town of Chard, the buildings of Forde Abbey still appear as a monastery unaltered since the Middle Ages. Set in deep countryside, and framed by a magnificent garden, the golden tones of the Ham Hill stone have a harmony about them that is rare in a building that has been occupied for more than four centuries. From the reign of Stephen, grandson of William the Conqueror, until the Dissolution in 1539, Forde Abbey was a Cistercian monastery. In 1141, Adelicia de Brioniis offered the Manor of Thorncombe a site beside the Axe for a new monastery, and within seven years the buildings were ready for occupation. The Abbey acquired a reputation for learning, and its third abbot was Baldwin, who became Archbishop of Canterbury and crowned Richard I.

Thomas Chard, the last abbot, ruled from 1521 until 1539, and during his time the buildings were restored with great splendour and magnificence. The great Perpendicular tower over the entrance porch was his, and he proudly recorded the date, 1528, and his own name on the tall oriel windows. After the Dissolution, the Abbey went through a period of decay until 1649, when Edmund Prideaux, Oliver Cromwell's Attorney General, bought Forde Abbey, and a new period of glory began. He changed the Abbot's lodging into private quarters for his family, shortening the Great Hall in the process, created a Grand Saloon out of the monks' gallery and added a series of state apartments over the cloister.

The Great Hall, with its magnificent oak-panelled roof, is a dignified Tudor room giving access to the Great Stair. Here, Prideaux's embellishments are obvious, with wonderful pierced foliage panels instead of baluster rails beneath a plaster ceiling. The saloon, famous for its plasterwork, is hung with Mortlake tapestries, commissioned by Prideaux and based on Raphael cartoons of the Acts of the Apostles.

FURSDON Devon

The Fursdon family have remained loyal to the home that bears their name, living in the manor since the 13th century and seldom leaving. In 1418 Robert Fursdon was in France with the army of Henry V, and in 1643 George Fursdon was killed fighting for Charles I. His shrewd and formidable widow, Grace, took over the management of the estate, continuing to run Fursdon even after her son came of age, and became a moneylender. She died in her eighties, worth £20,000. Another Fursdon bought himself a troop of Light Dragoons and saw service with the Duke of York in the Napoleonic wars, on one occasion giving up his horse when the royal steed was killed.

The 19th century saw a decline in the family fortune. George Fursdon was a gambler and, though his son secured himself an heiress, her father's bank went bankrupt. The family invested in a local copper mine that suffered the same fate and the last few servants left to fight in the Great War. The Fursdons stayed on, despite taxation and the problem of dry rot, and in recent years have reversed the tide by revitalizing the estate and by converting some wings of the house to holiday accommodation.

The present house is 400 years old, though it was altered in the 18th century, and its rooms are elegant but unpretentious. It is furnished largely in Georgian style, though the table in the dining room has been in the house since Tudor times. The Fursdon family have accumulated a fascinating array of treasures over the years, including portraits, historic costumes, mementoes, archives and bric-a-brac – a collection that celebrates the history of this English country family.

Fursdon is a fine old country house with mostly Georgian furnishings

HARTLAND ABBEY Devon

When the Augustinian monastery of Hartland was dissolved in 1539, Henry VIII gave it to the sergeant of his wine cellar, perhaps in jocular acknowledgement of his name – John Abbott. The Abbotts had family connections with Sir Richard Greville, the explorer and adventurer, whose great-grandson John became a hero of the Civil War when he was only twelve years old. The property subsequently passed by inheritance and marriage through the Luttrells and Orchards to the Stucley family, who are the present owners, but the monastic buildings were demolished in the 18th century and replaced with the Gothic-style mansion we see today.

The fascination of Hartland Abbey lies in its portrayal of Victorian high life, with photographs of Stucleys fighting for the Empire, shooting snipe and making social calls. The interior is High Victorian, with touches of Queen Anne. Murals in the dining room and inner hall, based upon designs found in the House of Lords, portray the historic exploits of the family. There are decorated ceilings and an extraordinary corridor commissioned by Sir George Stucley after visiting the Alhambra. And if all this inspires visions of heroics, romance and history, so much the better.

The contents of the house are varied and include a set of Meissen that belonged to Marie Antoinette, and old documents from the medieval abbey that were discovered in an ancient box. In one of them a farmer swears by the sacred relics of St Nestan to desist from kidnapping and harming the king's messengers!

The Upper Corridor leads the visitor to the Alhambra Corridor (left), which was part of the 18th-century house. The astonishing painted vault was created by Gilbert Scott in 1862. A display of pictures shows the Abbey as it was before it was remodelled in 1779

KNIGHTSHAYES COURT Devon

2 miles (3km) north of Tiverton at Bolham | Open mid February to late October | Tel: 01643 823004/821314 | **www.nationaltrust.org.uk**

Though principally famous for its wonderful gardens, Knightshayes Court is well worth a visit in its own right. Its foundation stone was laid in 1869 but it took so long for work to progress that the architect, William Burges, was sacked in 1874 and J D Crace was appointed to complete the decoration. His painted ceilings and wall stencilling, hidden by later decorations, were only recently uncovered and restored.

Many features installed by Burges also remain, including some delightfully whimsical corbel figures, wood panelling, a great painted bookcase in the stairwell and a series of architectural drawings. In fact, many of the rooms at Knightshayes are an amalgam of the styles of Burges and Crace, endowing them with a unique interest.

The house was built for John Heathcoat-Amory, MP for Tiverton, and remained in the family until the 3rd Baronet, Sir John, died in 1972, leaving the property to the National Trust. It contains a collection of Old Masters and some fine family portraits. Of particular interest is the Golf Room, which illustrates Lady Heathcoat-Amory's golfing career. As Miss Joyce Wethered, she was four-times winner of the Ladies Open in the 1920s.

Above: The south front of Knightshayes Court

Right: An ornate bedroom, recreated just as architect William Burges originally intended

LACOCK ABBEY Wiltshire

3 miles (5km) south of Chippenham | Open selected days January to December | Tel: 01249 730459 | **www.nationaltrust.org.uk**

When Lacock Abbey was given to the National Trust in 1944 it came with a whole village. The Abbey was founded in 1232 by Ela, Countess of Salisbury, who was married to William Longespee, the illegitimate son of Henry II. Built of stone from a quarry at Hazelbury, Wiltshire, and wood from the royal forests, the Abbey continued as an Augustinian nunnery until Henry VIII dissolved the monasteries in 1539. Like many other religious foundations, Lacock became a private residence, but many of its monastic buildings, including the cloisters, chapter house and sacristy, were retained and Lacock was converted with sensitivity, though some of its features are Gothic Revival rather than pure medieval. It is furnished with some interesting pieces, including a chair that is said to have been used in the camp of Charles I, and a pair of 18th-century leather chests. Also on display is a photographic copy of the Lacock Abbey Magna Carta.

For most of its secular life, Lacock Abbey was owned by the Talbots, whose most famous son was William Henry Fox Talbot (1900–77), the pioneer of photography and inventor of the photographic negative. The middle window in the south gallery was the subject of his earliest negative, and there is a Museum of Photography in the gatehouse.

Sunlight filters through the intricate fan tracery ceiling in the north walk of Lacock Abbey's cloisters

LANHYDROCK Cornwall

Lanhydrock could have looked very different to the lovely, symmetrical Tudor mansion ranged around three sides of a courtyard that we see today. The fact is that only the north wing, entrance porch and gatehouse are original. The rest of the 17th-century house was destroyed by fire in 1881, at a time when conservation of the past was often sacrificed to Victorian enthusiasms. Fortunately, the owner, Lord Robartes, had the house rebuilt in the exact style of the remaining portion, using the same grey granite and recreating what is one of the most delightful compositions in the country.

Inside, though, it is pure Victoriana and a tour of the house gives a vivid insight into the lives of both the owners and their staff. The 'below stairs' parts of the house include an enormous kitchen with larders and a dairy, still with the equipment and utensils required to feed a great household. The tour also includes the bakehouse, cellars and the servants' quarters. Of the grander apartments, the Long Gallery, in the original wing, is particularly splendid. It is 116 feet (35m) long and has an intricately carved plasterwork ceiling depicting scenes from the Old Testament, worked by local craftsmen in the mid-17th century. Throughout, the house is furnished in fine style with some lovely 18th-century furniture and tapestries.

The house was given to the National Trust in 1953, having belonged to the Robartes family since 1620. The gatehouse, a survivor from the original building, stands alone as the main entrance to the house and formal gardens. These cover some 22 acres (9ha) and consist of herbaceous borders and formal parterres, with clipped yews and bronze urns. There are also beautiful rhododendrons, camellias and magnolias.

The barrel-vaulted plaster ceiling of the Long Gallery (top) and the Luggage Room (right)

LONGLEAT Wiltshire

5 miles (8km) west of Warminster | Open daily end of March to October; selected days February and March | Tel: 01985 844400 | **www.longleat.co.uk**

From Heaven's Gate, the view of Longleat is unforgettable. The trees that line the drive suddenly draw back to reveal a panorama stretching to the distant Mendip Hills, and a swathe of open parkland drops down into the valley, with a haze of darker woods beyond. Central to this composition is the house itself. Longleat at this distance is like some palace from a fairytale. Honey-coloured stone and glass reflect the sun, while the turrets, cupolas and chimneys are mirrored in the waters of a lake.

Now famous above all things for its lions, Longleat was bought for £53 in 1541 by John Thynne, a young man who rapidly rose to wealth and power in that era. Assisted by mason Robert Smythson, sculptor Allen Maynard and joiner Adrian Gaunt, the result of this collaboration was a palace built to celebrate prosperity and peace, a modern home to suit a modern man. The site was chosen purely for its beauty, the house itself designed with no thought for defence, its great bayed walls of stone and mullioned glass setting a new trend in Elizabethan architecture. Thynne was a perfectionist who wanted the Gothic splendour of a Tudor mansion, yet loved the classical perfection of Italian architecture. He gave each floor pilasters in ascending order of Doric, Ionic and Corinthian; he made the house symmetrical with matching wings, yet on the roof he threw away all classic elegance for Tudor quirkiness by the addition of the 'banketting houses', where groups of friends might gather for an after-dinner drink.

The Golden Age of Longleat was in the reign of Queen Victoria and the interior remains a monument to this extraordinary period. Despite Reform Acts and a rising middle class, the English aristocracy had never been so confident; their estates were hugely profitable, their investments were secure, society was God-fearing and stable.

The Great Hall is the only room at Longleat that John Thynne would still recognize. High overhead, carved pendants hang from Tudor hammer beams and Queen Elizabeth I must have warmed herself before the huge carved chimneypiece. The state rooms are, by contrast, pure Victorian and extraordinary to modern eyes.

Lord Bath's apartments are a revelation: he has painted many of the walls with his own murals. Vast, exuberant and often of a most explicit nature, their lack of all restraint seems perfectly in keeping with the house.

Reflected in the lake, Longleat is a symmetrical three-storey house surrounded by glorious parkland

MONTACUTE HOUSE Somerset

4 miles (6.5km) west of Yeovil | Open March to end of October | Tel: 01935 823289 | www.nationaltrust.org.uk

Montacute is one of Britain's best-preserved Elizabethan mansions – an impressive edifice of glittering glass interspersed with the golden glow of Ham Hill stone. It was built around the end of the 16th century for Sir Edward Phelips, a lawyer who rose to be Speaker of the House of Commons and Master of the Rolls (it was he who opened for the Prosecution at the trial of Guy Fawkes).

The interior of the house is no less impressive than its beautiful, symmetrical exterior. There are decorated ceilings, splendidly ornate fireplaces, heraldic glass and fine wood panelling, but by the time the property came to the National Trust the original contents had, sadly, been dispersed. In fact, the house itself was nearly lost – in 1931, after years of neglect, it was on the market for £5,882 'for scrap'!

Rescue came in the form of a Mr E Cook who donated sufficient funds to buy Montacute and give it to the National Trust.

Montacute House's elegant drive is lined with clipped Irish yews, beeches, limes and oaks

Today, the rooms have been suitably furnished thanks to various loans and bequests, and the Long Gallery – at 172ft (52m) the largest surviving gallery in the country – houses a magnificent collection of Elizabethan and Jacobean paintings that are on permanent loan from the National Portrait Gallery.

31

NEWHOUSE Wiltshire

Newhouse was built in about 1619 as a hunting lodge for Sir Edward Gorges. Most unusual in design, it is built in the shape of a 'Y', perhaps to symbolize the Trinity – such 'devices' amused Jacobean architects, and Gorges's main house, Longford Castle, was constructed as a triangle. Sir Edward's fortune sank in the fens of Lincolnshire – or, at least, in a scheme to drain them – and Newhouse was subsequently sold to a family of prominent Cromwellians, the Eyres.

In the early 18th century Sir Robert Eyre became Chancellor to the Prince of Wales and Lord Chief Justice of the Court of Common Pleas. Alexander Pope said of him that 'the end of the world would come before a smile from Lord Chief Justice Eyre'. His son, a trustee of the colony of Georgia, installed a second staircase and added to the north-west wing, whilst the south-east was extended later in the 18th century to provide a splendid drawing room.

One daughter of the house was married to a cousin of Lord Nelson, and his child by Emma Hamilton, Horatia, was brought up by the family at Newhouse. Her cot, made by a ship's carpenter, can still be seen, as can a portrait of Lord Nelson as captain of

Once virtually derelict, Newhouse still retains its old wood panelling and other Jacobean features

the frigate *Albermarle*. The most intriguing painting in the house is undoubtedly the 'Hare Picture', which portrays a triumphant band of hares hunting and mercilessly slaughtering humans.

When it was inherited by the present owners in the early 1970s, Newhouse was virtually derelict and it has taken many years of work to restore it. The drawing room is Edwardian in decor, but Jacobean fireplaces and old panelling survive elsewhere.

PENCARROW HOUSE Cornwall

Pencarrow House, at the end of a mile-long woodland drive, has been the home of the Molesworth-St Aubyn family since the Elizabethan age. Its original owners, the de Pencarrow family, lost it after an abortive Cornish rising against an unjust levy on tin in 1497. The first Molesworth here was John, Queen Elizabeth's commissioner for the Duchy of Cornwall; his grandson Colonel Hender Molesworth governed Jamaica under Charles II and William III, and was created a baronet. It was, however, two 18th-century Molesworths who employed architect Robert Allanson to create the present house, with its Palladian-style entrance front. The long south front, with its roof of grey Delabole slate, has a Cornish feel, while the north-facing back of the house opens into a courtyard and was probably the main front of the earlier house.

A second stage in the development of Pencarrow occurred in 1841, when the 8th Baronet, Sir William, engaged a Plymouth architect, George Wightwick, to improve the interiors, one result being the particularly fine drawing room. Its beautiful rose-coloured damask curtains were a gift of a relative, Captain George Ourry, who took them as part of his booty from a Spanish ship, the *Santissima Trinidada*, which he captured off the Philippines in 1762.

As well as its fine furniture and ceramics, the house contains many family portraits, including that of the 18th-century Cornish MP Sir John Aubyn, identified by Prime Minister Walpole as the only MP he could not bribe. Another is of the 8th Baronet, who was Palmerston's Colonial Secretary, responsible for ending penal transportation to Australia.

The present owners take enormous pride in caring for the house, and have restored the neglected 19th-century woodlands.

The Palladian-style entrance front of Pencarrow House gives way to a charmingly furnished interior

POWDERHAM CASTLE Devon

The soaring towers of Powderham recall the age of chivalry in a manner totally appropriate to this most romantic house. Late in the 14th century the castle was constructed by Sir Philip Courtenay, a younger son of the Earl of Devon. The castle was besieged and damaged during the English Civil War, rebuilt in the 18th century and further changed by Wyatt in the 1790s. For centuries the Courtenays, though descended from a great historic family, prospered in a cautiously provincial manner, their only claim to notoriety being a youthful friendship between the 3rd Viscount and the wicked writer and art collector William Beckford. It was while in exile in New York and Paris in 1831 that the 3rd Viscount, William Courtenay, discovered from his son's researches into ancient documents that he was entitled to revive the Earldom of Devon, a title the family still holds today.

Powderham bears witness to the changing fortunes of the Courtenays. Its exterior is part medieval castle, part Gothic fantasy. The dining hall, though ancient in appearance, is in fact Victorian, with a splendidly romantic fireplace and coats of arms that proudly trace the Courtenay line back to the 11th century. Among the many other rooms, two are quite exceptional: Wyatt's music room, with a spectacular domed ceiling, and the staircase hall. The stairs themselves are grand and beautifully constructed, but the most amazing feature is the plasterwork. Birds and flowers, a cornucopia of fruit, even garden implements tumble in profusion against a bright blue background. The chapel too is interesting, converted from the grange of the medieval castle, with some fine old timbers in the roof. A house of many different styles and periods, Powderham is full of delights.

Powderham Castle's largely 19th-century exterior is full of Gothic delights and sumptuous furnishings

PRIDEAUX PLACE Cornwall

In the centre of Padstow | Open selected afternoons Easter to October for guided tours | Tel: 01841 532411 | www.prideauxplace.co.uk

The layout of Prideaux Place reflects its passage through the ages. Its E-shaped plan is Elizabethan, as is its massive oak front door and its crowning glory, the Great Chamber, with its superb plaster ceiling.

In the 18th-century Edmund Prideaux returned from his Grand Tour and removed the pointed gables on the entrance front, and installed sash windows and coal-burning grates. He also bought a whole room from Lord Bath's doomed Restoration manor house at Stow – panelling, pictures, wine cooler and all. But Edmund's restrained Georgian style did not satisfy the taste of his grandson, the Reverend Charles Prideaux, and in about 1810 the Reverend started applying the Regency Gothic style. His particular influence is reflected in the drawing room, hall and library.

Among the many fine paintings in the house are a group in the morning room by John Opie, who had grown up on the Prideaux estate before becoming a famous Regency court painter. The group includes a rare self-portrait, left as a 'tip' for the housekeeper. Perhaps the most romantic painting is that of Humphrey Prideaux, painted by the Italian artist, Rosalba Carriera.

She fell in love with him and hid a letter saying so in the frame of this picture. The letter was not discovered until 1914, so Humphrey never knew.

Prideaux Place has 81 rooms, 44 of them bedrooms, but of those bedrooms only six are habitable. The present owners, Peter and Elizabeth Prideaux-Brune, are restoring the house and garden, and delight in showing visitors around.

Elegance and symmmetry play their part in the architecture of this beautiful manor house in the centre of Padstow

ST MICHAEL'S MOUNT Cornwall

Open selected days from March to end of October | ½ mile (1km) offshore from Marazion | Tel: 01736 710507 | **www.stmichaelsmount.co.uk**

An old Cornish legend claims that in the 5th century some fishermen saw the Archangel St Michael on a ledge of rock on the western side of the Mount, and it has been called St Michael's Mount ever since.

Legends aside, this great rock is a picturesque sight. Perched upon its summit is a building that has been a church, a priory, a fortress and a private home. It was built in 1135 by the abbot of its namesake, Mont St Michel in Normandy, France, to whom it had been granted by the Norman Earl of Cornwall. However, the original building was destroyed by an earthquake in 1275.

For all its isolation, the Mount was seen as strategically important whenever there was turmoil in England – the Wars of the Roses, the Prayer Book Rebellion, the Armada and, of course, the Civil War, when it was a Royalist stronghold until surrendered to Parliament in 1646, and subsequently taken over as a garrison. When the military left, the Mount came into the private ownership of the St Aubyn family, and in the late 18th century, the family began to look upon the Mount as a more permanent residence.

Undaunted by the fact that the living quarters were not of an adequate size, they set about the construction of a new wing – not an easy task on a great rock that is cut off at every high tide.

The St Aubyns were obviously a force to be reckoned with, however, and the splendid Victorian apartments that they added are as much a testament to their determination as to their good taste. Inside the apartments there are some fine plaster reliefs, beautiful Chippendale furniture and collections of armour and pictures.

At low tide 12th-century St Michael's Mount is joined to the mainland by a causeway

SAND Devon

On his retirement in 1560, James Huyshe, a successful London grocer, purchased Sand, and his descendants still live there today. The present house was completed before 1600 by Rowland Huyshe and his wife Anne, whose initials are carved into a gable. In the Civil War the Huyshes, though Protestant in their beliefs, were staunch supporters of the Stuart cause, enduring fines and confiscations as a consequence. Both of their daughters, clearly girls of independent mind, married generals in Cromwell's army.

In the 18th century the fortunes of the Huyshes declined and Sand was let out as a farmhouse, though when a neighbour's gamekeeper dared to trespass on the property, the Reverend Francis Huyshe wrote furiously that it was 'the miserable remains of an old family estate, which will be defended with family pride.'

Sand was restored by Francis Huyshe early in the 20th century and although the house was subsequently let once more, the present owner, Colonel Huyshe, took up residence in 1967. Despite the many changes it has undergone, Sand still has Tudor fireplaces and old heraldic glass, and a staircase has survived from an even older house. A home that has adapted to the needs of modern life, Sand remains a relic of the squirearchy that seems, according to one visitor, 'to have grown out of the ground.'

Above: As its name implies, Sand is very much a part of the countryside that surrounds it

Left: The Edwardian cedar summerhouse

SHERBORNE CASTLE Dorset

On the eastern edge of Sherborne | Open selected days April to November | Tel: 01935 812072 | **www.sherbornecastle.com**

Sir Walter Raleigh first saw Sherborne when riding to his fleet at Plymouth and – the story goes – was so enchanted by the view that he tumbled from his horse. Encouraged by a gift of jewellery from Raleigh, Queen Elizabeth put pressure on the owner, the Bishop of Salisbury, to relinquish the estate.

Raleigh first attempted modernizing the old Norman castle, but later switched attention to a site across the River Yeo. Newly married and already with a son, he planned a home for his family and a refuge from his dangerous, fast life. In the grounds he laid out water gardens and a bowling green, planting trees from the New World, with a stone bench beneath their shade.

Raleigh's life here was unorthodox and there were rumours of black masses in the tower study. Cleared on a charge of atheism, but bored with country life, Raleigh led an expedition up the Orinoco, returning sadder and no richer to the home he loved 'above all his possessions, of all places on earth.'

Since 1617 the Digbys have owned Sherborne, many of them matching Raleigh in bravery and individualism. John, later 1st Earl of Bristol, was given the estate by King James I for his attempts to negotiate a Spanish marriage for Prince Charles.

Sherborne Castle is larger than it was in Raleigh's time, but his square Elizabethan house remains central. Most of the interior was refurbished in the 18th and the 19th centuries. The light and airy Gothic library is particularly pretty; other rooms are much grander, designed for entertaining royalty. Many of the fireplaces and elaborate ceilings bear the Digby crest of a heraldic ostrich.

'Capability' Brown's grounds maximize the setting; Raleigh's cedars are still growing and his bench is still a great vantage point.

Sherborne Castle looks every bit as enchanting today as it did in Sir Walter Raleigh's time

STANWAY HOUSE Gloucestershire

10 miles (16km) west of Stow-on-the-Wold | Open selected afternoons June, July and August | Tel: 01386 584528 | www.stanwayfountain.co.uk

Nestling deep in the glorious Gloucestershire countryside at the edge of the Cotswolds is Stanway House, one of Britain's most romantic Jacobean manor houses. It was built between 1590 and 1630 in mellow golden limestone by the Tracys, a family that had owned land in the county since the Conquest. The manor was given by two Mercian magnates to the Abbey of Tewkesbury as its first endowment, and it was on the Dissolution of the Monasteries that Stanway changed hands for the only time in 1,270 years when Richard Tracy obtained a lease of the property with the assistance of Thomas Cromwell.

Approaching the house from the beautiful village of Stanway, you pass the magnificent 14th-century tithe barn built by the Abbey, and also the charming, jewel-like gatehouse, which dates from around 1630. The facade is dominated by the splendid gables and by the magnificent tall windows that give light to the Great Hall. Beyond the screens passage the hall still possesses an unmistakable Elizabethan atmosphere, with a raised dais at one end and at the other a minstrels' gallery, now made into a bedroom above the screen. The Audit Room has a rent table of 1780, where the estate still receives payment in person from its tenants, while steps from the Great Hall lead up to the Great Parlour.

Surrounded by ancient parkland, the water garden is one of the finest in England.

The gatehouse (below) and the drawing room (right)

SUDELEY CASTLE Gloucestershire

Set in deeply wooded countryside, Sudeley Castle incorporates the remains of a medieval castle. Some of 15th-century Sudeley is in ruins, having been 'slighted' by Parliamentary forces during the Civil War, but the mellow stone of the banqueting hall, the tithe barn and the dungeon tower remain. Henry VIII is believed to have visited the castle with Anne Boleyn in 1532. After Henry's death, it became the home of his widow, Katherine Parr, when she married Sir Thomas Seymour in 1547. Among the large retinue that the Queen Dowager brought to Sudeley was the ill-fated Lady Jane Grey.

After a long period of neglect, Sudeley was bought in 1830 by brothers, William and John Dent, from a rich family of Worcester glovers. After their deaths, the castle was inherited by their cousin, John Coucher Dent, whose wife Emma devoted her life to the enrichment of Sudeley. With the help of the architect Sir George Gilbert Scott, who designed the beautiful tomb of Katherine Parr in the church, the house was restored.

Entry to the castle apartments is through the Rent Room, where the agent would have collected the tenants' payments, and the North Hall, once the guardroom. This room displays a fine portrait of Charles I by Van Dyck. In the Queen's Bedroom is the remarkable allegorical painting by Lucas de Heere, Chudleigh. Blatantly political, it shows Queen Elizabeth I surrounded by the goddesses of peace and plenty, while, in

The award-winning gardens and mellow stone walls of Sudeley Castle are steeped in history

marked contrast, her predecessor, Queen Mary, is depicted with her husband, Philip of Spain, and Mars, the Roman god of war.

Among the relics of Queen Katherine Parr are her prayer book and a love letter to Seymour accepting his proposal of marriage. From the period of the Civil War, there is a display of armour discovered during excavations, as well as a fascinating letter from Charles I to the freeholders of Cornwall.

Sudeley Castle's gardens were laid out during the 19th-century restoration, with fine terraces and spectacular views over the ancient trees in the Home Park.

UGBROOKE PARK Devon

9 miles (14km) south west of Exeter | Open selected afternoons July to September | Tel: 01626 852179 | www.ugbrooke.co.uk

An ancient and romantic family, the Cliffords claim descent from Viking kings and Dukes of Normandy. Arriving in this country with the Conquest, they played their part as warriors and barons in every conflict of the age. Roger fought for both sides in the Barons' War, Robert died at Bannockburn, his son was hanged at York after Lancaster's rebellion, and John, the 9th Baron, earned the nickname 'the butcher' for his ferocity in the Wars of the Roses.

A medieval house at Ugbrooke belonging to the Precentor of the diocese of Exeter was seized by Protector Somerset. Rebuilt as a Tudor manor, it passed through marriage to the Cliffords late in the 16th century. Though at first the poor relations of the family, the Chudleigh Cliffords rose to fame in the reign of Charles II, when Thomas, the first Lord Clifford, a hero of the war with Holland, became treasurer of the royal household. Well-meaning but incompetent, his downfall came in opposing Parliament when his opponents passed the Test Act to exclude all Roman Catholics from office.

Ugbrooke was remodelled in the 18th century by Robert Adam, who paid tribute to the Cliffords' war-like heritage in the 'castle' style that he adopted, with battlemented towers at each corner of the mansion. The park was transformed by 'Capability' Brown, with a long, narrow lake the central feature of a gently rolling landscape. After World War II, Ugbrooke was neglected, with many of its finest rooms used for storing grain, but the house has now been restored. The library is a splendid Adam room, its plasterwork and colour scheme exactly as they were 200 years ago. The house contains some fine old silver, tapestries and paintings, with an unexpected bonus in the chapel. Designed by Adam in a dramatic style, with a vaulted apse and open balconies, its marble columns, painted panels and elaborate decoration have an almost Byzantine richness.

The elegant facade of Ugbrooke House, seen across the cow parsley-fringed lake

Whittington Court stands on the western edge of the Cotswolds above Cheltenham. The moat that surrounded the property still runs along two sides of the south garden. Whittington Church, probably once its private chapel, stands close by and contains family memorials, including a brass to Richard Cotton (died 1556), for whom the house was built. The original plan was E-shaped, but during its history the porch was moved to the eastern end of the Great Hall and the present cross wing was rebuilt in the 17th century.

Although Whittington Court seems to be a house of the 16th and 17th centuries, its origins lie much deeper in history. Probably named Witetune in Anglo-Saxon times, the manor of Whittington belonged to the de Crupe family in the Middle Ages, and there are tombs to three members of the family in the 12th-century church. Later it was owned by the Despencer family who were Earls of Gloucester, and after the death of the great Earl of Warwick, his widow, Anne, was persuaded to transfer Whittington to King Henry VII.

In 1545 the manor came into the hands of the Cotton family, and it was John Cotton who had the privilege of entertaining Queen Elizabeth at Whittington during a progress she made through Gloucestershire in 1592.

Built of ashlar stone, Whittington Court is an Elizabethan manor house near the site of a Roman villa

Records state that she 'dyned at Mr Coton's at Whytinton'. The manor later passed to Ann Cotton, who was married to Sir John Denham, a courtier, poet and dilettante architect who, at the Restoration, was given the post of Surveyor-General of the King's Works. It is likely that his influence was brought to bear on some of the classical features added to the house in that period. The Grand Staircase has an original 17th-century dog gate on the first half-landing to prevent dogs from going to the bedrooms.

WILTON HOUSE Wiltshire

3 miles (5km) west of Salisbury | Open selected days April to end of August | Tel: 01722 746714 | www.wiltonhouse.com

Few houses match Wilton in the richness of their history. An extraordinary family – ancestors of Sir William Herbert – have played host here to sovereigns and the brightest figures of each reign. The house is fascinating for its architecture, incorporating Tudor elements, the masterpiece of Jones and Webb and the Gothicism of James Wyatt, with the finest bridge in England in its grounds. The state rooms in themselves are worth a detour. Some may find them ostentatious, but they successfully contrive to achieve a balance between baroque vulgarity and predictable good taste.

Like many of England's great country houses, Wilton is built upon monastic ruins. More than a thousand years ago the Wessex kings held court here and it was probably King Alfred who gave the palace to the Benedictine nuns. At one time the abbey was among the richest in England, but it had declined considerably by 1539, when the King's men seized the estate.

Outside, Wilton House presents a dignified, restrained appearance to the world, in keeping with an age of sober dress and outward gravity. What is found inside is altogether something else. The drama builds up gradually, through ante-rooms of mounting splendour to the glories of the Single Cube, followed by the still more dazzling Double Cube, created by Inigo Jones and Webb, circa 1653. This is a room that takes the breath away, both by its scale and through the richness of its decoration, its pale painted walls backdrops to a blaze of colour. Gilded swags and garlands, cornices and pediments create an impression of exuberant indulgence.

The elegant south front of Wilton House, built between 1636 and 1640

If the rooms at Wilton are sumptuous, then so are the contents of the house – collections built up through the centuries by individuals whose skill in recognizing excellence has been well matched by their ability to pay for it. As well as the Van Dycks, every room contains magnificent Old Masters by Rembrandt, Van Leyden and Jan Breughal, portraits by Reynolds and Lely, landscapes and sporting scenes. One of the most disturbing paintings is a portrait by an unknown artist of the homicidal 7th Earl of Pembroke, tense and restless as he turns, or possibly rips out, the pages of a book.

The little ante-room (above) and the north cloister (right) added between 1801 and 1815

In the entrance hall a larger-than-life statue of William Shakespeare has greeted Wilton's visitors since the 9th Earl paid £100 to have him made, commemorating, in a somewhat stilted form, the bard's great debt of gratitude to Herbert generosity. Wonderfully unsubtle, it introduces all the grandeur of the palace in a way that makes such splendour understandable; the overpowering desire to be revered and remembered by future generations.

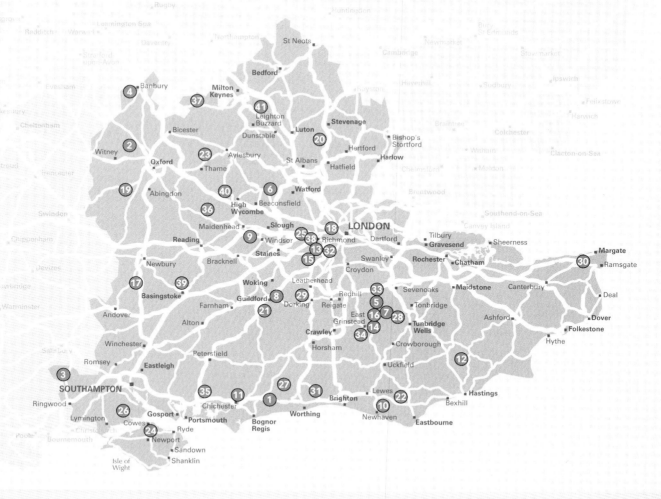

1	**Arundel Castle** West Sussex	50
15	**Hampton Court** Surrey	65
29	**Polesden Lacey** Surrey	81

2	**Blenheim Palace** Oxfordshire	51
16	**Hever Castle** Kent	66
30	**Quex Park** Kent	82

3	**Breamore House** Hampshire	52
17	**Highclere Castle** Berkshire	67
31	**St Mary's House** West Sussex	83

4	**Broughton Castle** Oxfordshire	53
18	**Kensington Palace** London	68
32	**Southside House** London	84

5	**Chartwell** Kent	54
19	**Kingston Bagpuize** Oxfordshire	69
33	**Squerryes Court** Kent	85

6	**Chenies Manor House** Hertfordshire	55
20	**Knebworth House** Hertfordshire	70
34	**Standen** West Sussex	86

7	**Chiddingstone Castle** Kent	56
21	**Loseley House** Surrey	71
35	**Stansted Park** West Sussex	88

8	**Clandon Park** Surrey	57
22	**Michelham Priory** East Sussex	72
36	**Stonor Park** Oxfordshire	89

9	**Dorney Court** Berkshire	58
23	**Nether Winchendon House** Bucks	73
37	**Stowe House & Gardens** Bucks	90

10	**Firle Place** East Sussex	59
24	**Osborne House** Isle of Wight	74
38	**Syon House** Middlesex	92

11	**Goodwood House** West Sussex	60
25	**Osterley** Middlesex	76
39	**The Vyne** Hampshire	93

12	**Great Dixter** East Sussex	61
26	**Palace House, Beaulieu** Hampshire	78
40	**West Wycombe Park** Bucks	94

13	**Ham House** Surrey	62
27	**Parham Park** West Sussex	79
41	**Woburn Abbey** Bedfordshire	95

| 14 | **Hammerwood Park** West Sussex | 64 |
| 28 | **Penshurst Place** Kent | 80 |

SOUTH & SOUTH EAST ENGLAND | 2

The area of England closest to London has always attracted the rich and powerful, so it is unsurprising that so many historic houses cluster in this region. Today it holds the palatial ducal mansions of the dukes of Norfolk at Arundel, the Marlboroughs at Blenheim, the Bedfords at Woburn and the Richmonds at Goodwood, while the dukes of Northumberland treasure the superb Robert Adam state rooms of Syon House. On a more modest scale is The Vine at Basingstoke, and other historic homes are filled with memories – of Henry VIII and Anne Boleyn at Hever Castle, of a king's mistress and the first pineapple at Dorney Court, of Princess Diana at Kensington Palace. For the exotic, Japanese armour is alarmingly ensconced in Chiddingstone Castle, big game trophies at Quex Park and memories of Tutankhamun's tomb at Highclere Castle, while architectural pleasures run all the way from Tudor charm at Chenies Manor to the High Victorian romanticism of Knebworth House.

ARUNDEL CASTLE West Sussex

In Arundel | **Open selected days from April to October** | **Tel: 01903 882173** | **www.arundelcastle.org**

The gargantuan Barons' Hall of Arundel Castle is a suitably grand tribute to the two great families that have owned the fortress for the last 700 years and more: the Fitzalans, earls of Arundel, followed by the Howards, dukes of Norfolk and earls marshal of England.

The castle was founded soon after the Battle of Hastings by the Norman warlord, Roger of Montgomery. The 12th-century oval keep, perched on its high mound, is where the medieval lords of the castle and their families lived; the gateway through which visitors enter the castle is also medieval.

Almost everything else that meets the eye is more recent. The castle was badly knocked about in the 1640s, during the Civil War. The 8th and 11th Dukes began rebuilding in the 18th century, but were outdone by the 15th Duke, a formidable builder who succeeded to the title in 1860 as a boy of thirteen.

The castle's riches include Tudor furniture, armour, tapestries and clocks, and paintings by Van Dyck, Lely, Reynolds, Gainsborough, Lawrence, Opie, Millais and de Laszlo. As hereditary Earls Marshal, the dukes are responsible for the organization of coronations and other major occasions of state, and their baton of office can be seen. There are 10,000 volumes in the remarkable library, hushed and cool under its vaulted ceiling and solemn in dark mahogany.

For 500 years the Fitzalans and Howards have been laid to rest in the Fitzalan Chapel, which is a rarity – a Roman Catholic chapel in an Anglican parish church, from which it is separated by glass walls. The church was built in the 14th century by one of the Fitzalan Earls of Arundel.

A familiar sight in the town of Arundel, the castle occupies a suitably commanding position

BLENHEIM PALACE Oxfordshire

The story of Blenheim Palace began when a humble military man, John Churchill, married the future Queen Anne's lady-in-waiting and confidante, Sarah Jennings. As soon as Anne became queen in 1702, she gave Churchill the title Duke of Marlborough. His career was a triumph, with a string of spectacular victories in the War of Spanish Succession. The first was over France and Bavaria in the Battle of Blenheim in 1704. In recognition of the nation's gratitude, Anne gave him the manor of Woodstock and the money to build a grand house. John Vanbrugh, the architect, designed a main block surmounted by four towers, with two projecting wings, which earned it the nickname of Blenheim Castle.

Blenheim forms a series of theatrical settings, and its facade is a magnificent sight. From the central block, curved walls lead to the east and west wings. As you enter through the east gateway, look out for the carvings of the English lion strangling the French cockerel. Inside, there is another reference to the Battle of Blenheim on the 67 foot- (20m-) high ceiling of the marbled Great Hall, in the oval painting by Sir James Thornhill. In 1874, in a small, plain bedroom, Jenny Churchill gave birth to a son, Winston. Winston's father, Lord Randolph Spencer-Churchill, briefly became Chancellor of the Exchequer, but his son was to achieve far greater fame through his dogged leadership of Britain during World War II. A nearby exhibition about this imposing man includes a set of his young curls, and a maroon velvet boiler suit that he wore during the war, together with some of his oil paintings. Winston Churchill was born at Blenheim by chance (he was premature), but he maintained a great affection for the place, and is buried at nearby Bladon churchyard.

The beautifully proportioned Long Library at Blenheim Palace is just one of many sumptuous rooms

BREAMORE HOUSE Hampshire

3 miles (5km) north of Fordingbridge | Open: selected afternoons April to September | Tel: 01725 512468 | **www.breamorehouse.com**

Breamore House lies in a picturesque secluded farmland setting, little changed in over 400 years. It has been owned by the Hulse family for nine generations, since its purchase in 1748 by Edward Hulse, Physician to Queen Anne, George I and George II.

The Tudor character of the house is immediately apparent in the dining room, with heavy oak furniture and a large stone fireplace. In the Great Hall is a Van Dyck painting of Charles I's children and a charming full-length portrait of Charles II as a boy. The favourite painting of many visitors, however, is the village inn scene, *The Coming of the Storm*, by David Teniers. Teniers also designed the two superb Brussels tapestries (c.1630) here. The Netherlands connection continues in the Blue Drawing Room, with some immaculate Dutch marquetry furniture, the dowry of the beautiful Hannah Vanderplank, who married Edward Hulse III in 1741, and whose portrait is also here.

The West Drawing Room contains probably the most memorable painting in the house: *The Boy with the Bat*, from the mid-18th century, is one of the earliest paintings of cricket and has been exhibited internationally. More fine pictures line the Inner Hall. Lucas's sketch of the Duke of Wellington was the Duke's own favourite of all his many portraits, and a Canaletto hangs next to some acclaimed eye-witness battle paintings by Napoleon's war artist, Beaufort.

The Breamore Countryside Museum provides a splendid evocation of village life of the past, with recreations including a farmworker's cottage, smithy, wheelwright's shop, and dairy. There is also an important collection of tractors and steam engines, horse-drawn vehicles and fire-fighting equipment to wander around.

Heavy oak furniture (left) adds to Breamore House's essentially Tudor character (top)

52

BROUGHTON CASTLE Oxfordshire

3 miles (5km) south west of Banbury | Open selected afternoons April to September | Tel: 01295 276070 | **www.broughtoncastle.com**

Broughton is a castle in name only, for it is really an early 14th-century mansion, later enhanced by Tudor architects. It was built by Sir John de Broughton, who enlarged an existing building within the moat to form a manor house. Since 1370, however, it has been in the Fiennes family, and it was Richard Fiennes who in 1554 altered the property to meet the 'Court' style of Edward VI. He put in two floors above the Great Hall, two staircase projections to the south and added a pair of rooms to form the west wing, building on the foundations of a medieval kitchen. His son Richard embellished the interior, including the magnificent plaster ceiling in the Great Parlour, finishing the job in 1599.

Little has changed at Broughton since then. It escaped a Regency 'restoration' because the 15th Baron frittered away the family fortune as a member of the set of the Prince Regent and Count d'Orsay. The family left Broughton, and in 1837 sold off its contents, including the swans on the moat.

The 'Gothick' ceiling pendants in the Great Hall are one of the few 19th-century additions. A stone staircase leads to a rare 14th-century private chapel with its fixed altar slab. Queen Anne's Room is named after Anne of Denmark, wife of James I, who slept here in 1604. She is likely to have admired the exuberant plasterwork ceiling in the Great Parlour, completed five years previously. Broughton has two notable chimney-pieces: the one in Queen Anne's Room dates from at least 1551, possibly earlier; the other, of stone and stucco, in the Fontainebleau style, is in the King's Chamber, off the gallery. In addition to the family portraits, including one of William Fiennes, the splendidly panelled Oak Room has a painting of Mrs Nathaniel

Fiennes. Her daughter was Celia Fiennes, who became famous for the journals of her travels around England towards the end of the 17th century.

The Lady's Garden (below) and the mansion surrounded by its splendid swan-filled moat (bottom)

CHARTWELL Kent

2 miles (3km) south of Westerham | Open selected days March to August | Tel: 01732 866368 | www.nationaltrust.org.uk

In 1924 Sir Winston Churchill, then Chancellor of the Exchequer in the Conservative government, moved with his family to Chartwell – a modest Victorian house with magnificent views over the Weald of Kent – and it was to remain their home for the next forty years. It has become one of the most popular of the National Trust's properties – closer, perhaps, to visitors' own aspirations than any great palace, and certainly of immense interest as the home of one of our greatest statesmen.

At Chartwell, Churchill turned his hand to many things, not only the painting and writing for which he is well known, but also the creation, with his own hands, of the garden walls, rockeries and waterworks, and even the large swimming pool. Today the rooms of the house remain very much as they were in Churchill's day, including his studio containing many of his paintings, and his study, in which he did most of his writing.

The Museum and Uniform Rooms contain a selection of his uniforms and many awards

and gifts, as well as a 'wanted, dead or alive' poster issued after his escape from a Boer prison in 1899. Elsewhere around the house

The south front (left) and study (above) at Chartwell, home of Sir Winston Churchill between 1922 and 1964

are reminders of the great man and his interests – old cigar boxes, a painting of his most successful racehorse, the visitors book recording the great and the famous who came to Chartwell between 1924 and 1964, and portraits of family and friends.

CHENIES MANOR HOUSE Hertfordshire

2 miles (3km) north-west of Rickmansworth | Open selected afternoons April to October | Tel: 01494 762888 | www.cheniesmanorhouse.co.uk

The world-renowned garden at Chenies Manor perfectly complements the medieval manor house

Chenies Manor House, on the edge of a Chiltern village above the little River Chess, is a mellow brick Tudor house full of the idiosyncrasies of a house altered and matured over centuries. It has a secret chamber (possibly for hiding priests), tunnels running from the house to a nearby wood, a medieval well, rooms stayed in by Queen Elizabeth I and a ghost who may or may not be that of Henry VIII.

Built around two courtyards, the house is approached by a lime-tree-canopied forecourt alongside the parish church. Its oldest part, T-shaped and dating from around 1460, centres on a battlemented tower. The 'new' lodgings were added in the 1520s to provide better accommodation for guests, and the same era saw the installation of the fireplaces and spectacular brick Tudor chimneys, of which more than twenty survive. It is said that Henry VIII so admired them that he had the same craftsmen work on Hampton Court, which he was then in the process of enlarging.

Queen Elizabeth's room, where she probably held court on her frequent visits, is an oak-floored parlour with 16th-century tapestries and furniture from the 17th century. The State Bedroom, where she is believed to have slept, is hung with family portraits; it is now used as a billiards room. Another room full of history is the armoury – a primitive 140 foot- (43m-) long gallery on the top floor, where Roundhead soldiers were reputedly quartered during the English Civil War.

The house's present owners take pleasure in welcoming visitors personally. Outside they have recreated a turf labyrinth, as depicted in a 16th-century picture which is now at Woburn Abbey, and established a physic garden of medicinal herbs.

CHIDDINGSTONE CASTLE Kent

10 miles (16km) south west of Sevenoaks | Open selected days Easter to September | Tel: 01892 870347 | **www.chiddingstonecastle.org.uk**

The White Rose Drawing Room at Chiddingstone Castle

In a village full of wonderfully preserved Tudor houses, owned by the National Trust and frequently used in period films, lies Chiddingstone Castle. In earlier days it belonged to the Streatfeild family, rich local ironmasters. Henry Streatfeild employed the architect William Atkinson to turn the house into a mock-medieval castle. Atkinson's plans were, in fact, a scaled-down version of Scone Palace in Scotland, which he was building for the Karl of Mansfield, but Henry Streatfeild had overstretched himself financially, and the building work was halted with only the north and south wings completed. However, some cottages were demolished, simply because

they spoiled the view, and a lake was installed, which is now popular with anglers. A bream of famously colossal proportions was caught there in 1945.

The Streatfeilds eventually found the house too expensive to keep up and Colonel Sir Henry Streatfeild sold it in 1938. Troops were billeted there during the war, leaving it in a very sorry state, and it was later used as a school. By the time that the late Denys Eyre Bower bought the house in 1955 it was in a bad way. Mr Bower, originally from Derbyshire, had been an obsessive and eccentric collector since his teenage years – all the works of art displayed in the castle

today were collected by him. He worked as a bank clerk, but spent so much time collecting antiques that he was first moved to an obscure country branch then finally forced to leave. He set up in London as an antique dealer. Denys Bower died in 1977, leaving everything to the nation, and it was his hope that the castle and contents would be preserved intact – as they have been. There's a portrait of him in the study, along with Chinese porcelain, Derbyshire landscapes, the bust of an Egyptian pharoah and the drawings chest of the great engineer Telford.

56

CLANDON PARK Surrey

Tours of this superb Palladian mansion generally begin with its most notable feature: the magnificent two-storey Marble Hall with its superb plaster ceiling featuring astonishing figures whose legs protrude from the plasterwork and hang down quite realistically over the classical entablature.

The house was built by the Venetian architect Giacomo Leoni in about 1731 for the second Lord Onslow, and the series of rooms open to the public are beautifully proportioned and splendidly furnished, although when the National Trust acquired the house it was empty. The contents we see today are the result of a generous bequest by Mrs David Gubbay of Little Trent Park in Hertfordshire. Mrs Gubbay's legacy included the wonderful collection of porcelain, on display all around the house, the highlights of which include the extraordinarily delicate Commedia dell' Arte figures and a unique and colourful assortment of 17th- and 18th-century Chinese birds. The furniture includes some outstanding examples of marquetry work and there is some fine needlework on display.

In the grounds, don't miss the secluded sunken Dutch garden or the delightful Maori House, brought over from New Zealand in 1892 and the only historic Maori meeting house (*whare nui*) in the United Kingdom. Also at Clandon Park is the Museum of the Queen's Royal Surrey Regiment.

The east front at Clandon Park, built around 1731 by Venetian architect Giacomo Leoni

DORNEY COURT Berkshire

3 miles (5km) north west of Windsor | Open selected afternoons in May and June | Tel: 01628 604638 | www.dorneycourt.co.uk

Dorney Court is the quintessential English Tudor house. Built between 1440 and 1480, it is a picture-postcard property of blushing pink bricks, ancient timbered gables and soaring slender chimneys. The setting is an Anglo-Saxon idyll. Despite its proximity to bustling Windsor, the ancient meadowland of Dorney Common has a wild and timeless air, while the house is surrounded by hedges.

The Palmer family have lived at Dorney since 1620, with an unbroken lineage from father to son. There have been some notable ladies too, including the pretty Barbara Palmer, Countess of Castlemaine, who was a favourite mistress of Charles II.

In the Great Chamber the barrel-vaulted ceiling is said to be held up only by ancient branches that creak and groan with the house and often bring down plaster. The panelled bedroom walls slope at a drunken angle, and the last of the bedrooms, the Little Room, is haunted by a female form who points enigmatically to a panel in the wall.

Adjacent to the William-and-Mary-style dining room is the Great Hall, and the many portraits around the walls contain works by Kneller and Lely. There is also a rare set of Turkish portraits, brought to Dorney by Sir Roger Palmer, then Ambassador to the East for Charles II. The most curious piece is a large carved stone pineapple. It is said that Charles II gave Sir Roger the top of a Barbados pineapple. He planted this at Dorney and it became the first-ever pineapple to be grown in England. The fruit was presented to Charles II in 1661.

Dorney Court's rooms chronicle the evolution of the squirearchy in English country life

FIRLE PLACE East Sussex

5 miles (8km) south east of Lewes | Open selected afternoons from June until the end of September | Tel: 01273 858307 | www.firle.com

A line of great houses and stately parks lies beneath the northern slope of the South Downs in Sussex, and Firle is the easternmost. The Gage family have been notable collectors and the house is a living gallery of the lives and tastes of successive generations. Today's Georgian mansion conceals an older Tudor house. This was enlarged by Sir John Gage, a distinguished soldier and leading light of the court of Henry VIII. He commanded against the Scots in 1542, when King James V of Scotland was killed at Solway Moss. He was also Constable of the Tower of London, which gave him the disagreeable duty of superintending the executions of Queen Catherine Howard and Lady Jane Grey; the future Queen Elizabeth I spent a period in the Tower under his stern eye. His son, Sir Edward, as Sheriff of Sussex, oversaw the burning of the Lewes Martyrs, but later, as staunch Roman Catholics, the family had to retire from public life, and their house was often searched for concealed priests and weapons. In the 18th century Sir William Gage conformed to the Church of England and he and his cousin and successor, Sir Thomas, rebuilt the house in Palladian style with rococo elaborations.

Items of special American interest in the house come through General Thomas Gage, younger brother of the 2nd Viscount. A career soldier, he served gallantly against

Firle Place is surrounded by 150 acres of stunning parkland, including a picturesque lake

the French in North America and married an American, Margaret Kemble of Morristown, New Jersey. He was in command in Boston in 1775 and his men's skirmish with the rebellious colonists at Lexington was the first encounter of the War of Independence.

A feature of the house is one of the finest Georgian staircases in the country and a splendid collection of Old Masters, which includes works by Van Dyck, Fra Bartolomeo, Reynolds, Lawrence, Gainsborough and Rubens, as well as Sèvres porcelain and French and English furniture.

59

GOODWOOD HOUSE West Sussex

Nestled at the foot of the South Downs, Goodwood House is indeed glorious, both outside and in

Famous for its racecourse, Goodwood is the Sussex home of the Dukes of Richmond and Gordon, romantically descended on the wrong side of the blanket from King Charles II. The 1st Duke of Richmond, Charles Lennox, was his illegitimate son by the fascinating Louise de Keroualle, who was sent to England by Louis XIV as a spy.

The unusual flint house was originally a hunting lodge, bought by the 1st Duke in 1697. It was rebuilt in an H-shape in the 1760s for the 3rd Duke by Sir William Chambers (the architect of Somerset House in London) and altered at the end of the century by James Wyatt, who added towers at the corners as part of an expensive and abhortive plan to enlarge the building into a giant octagon. It was the 3rd Duke (whose debts were titanic) who collected the superb Sèvres porcelain and French furniture while

Ambassador in Paris. He also built kennels of unrivalled comfort for his hounds and initiated the horse races up on the Downs, which developed into 'Glorious Goodwood'.

His nephew and successor, the 4th Duke, was a friend of the great Duke of Wellington, who attended the Duchess of Richmond's famous ball on the eve of the Battle of Waterloo (there is a painting of the occasion in the house). In the early years of this century King Edward VII enjoyed banquets given in Goodwood's ballroom for the race meeting, and the present royal family have frequently been entertained here.

Successive dukes collected treasures that include magnificent Van Dycks of the royal Stuarts, Canalettos, horse pictures by Stubbs, Louis XV and Louis XVI furniture, 18th-century Gobelin tapestries, and elegant Chelsea porcelain.

10 miles (16km) north west of Rye | Open selected afternoons April to September | Tel: 01797 252878 | www.greatdixter.co.uk

Great Dixter is best known for its garden, but the house is a treat as well, with its crazily tilted porch and spacious Great Hall. Like other houses in this area, where there is little stone for building, it was constructed (in about 1460) of oak timbers filled in with lath and plaster. The household lived together in the Great Hall, a huge room open to the roof some 30 feet (9m) above, through which the smoke from the central hearth filtered out. Its combination of tie beams and hammer beams, some of which are carved with coats of arms, is unique.

Great Dixter was in a run-down state in 1910 when it was bought by Nathaniel Lloyd, a printer. He called in Sir Edwin Lutyens to restore the house and the hall was opened up to the roof again. As restoration cut down the amount of living space, Mr Lloyd spent £70 on another old hall-house, nine miles (14km) away at Benenden, which was taken down, brought over to Dixter in numbered sections and reconstructed there, while Lutyens added a new building of his own in a suitable vernacular idiom to connect the two. Lutyens also designed new gardens, and the result is altogether a delight.

Nathaniel Lloyd died in 1933, after which Great Dixter occupied much of the lives of his sons Christopher and Quentin, both born in the house. Christopher Lloyd (1921–2006), the well-known gardening writer, became a life member of the Royal Horticultural Society at the age of five and his many articles and books – including *The Year at Great Dixter* (1987) – helped make Dixter a household name among lovers of beautiful gardens. Laid out on the site of the farmyards, the gardens incorporate many of the original farm buildings, including an oasthouse, which was last used for drying hops in 1939.

Colourful plants in the cottage-style garden at Great Dixter, these days more famous than the house itself

HAM HOUSE Surrey

Between Richmond and Kingston-upon-Thames | **Open selected afternoons February to October** | **Tel: 020 8940 1950** | **www.nationaltrust.org.uk**

Ham House is an outstanding Stuart mansion that has managed to avoid the changes in architectural fashion that have altered so many of its contemporaries over the years. It was built in 1610 on the south bank of the Thames in the days when the river was the major thoroughfare into the city, giving its owner – Sir Tomas Vavasour, Knight Marshall of the King's Household to James – essential access to the royal households.

In 1626 Ham became home to William Murray, who had been the 'whipping boy' for the future Charles I and came to share his tastes in art and architecture. These were expressed in his remodelling of the interior of Ham between 1637 and 1639, when he created the Great Staircase and a number of grand rooms on the first floor. Some of Murray's art collection remains in the house, and offers a fascinating insight into the fashions of the period.

After Murray's death the house passed to his daughter, Elizabeth, who became Countess of Dysart. Described as beautiful, ambitious and greedy, she married first a wealthy and cultivated squire, Sir Lionel Tollemache, of Helmingham Hall in Suffolk. They had eleven children, of whom five survived to adulthood. Tollemache died in 1669 and Elizabeth then married John Maitland, 1st Duke of Lauderdale and Secretary of State for Scotland. The couple enlarged and redecorated the house in the most fashionable style, and much of their work is evident today. Even some of the furniture, specially made for the house in the 17th century, remains in situ.

It is likely that we have the Duchess of Lauderdale's extravagance to thank because she left her descendant decidedly short of any funds that might have been used to make alterations. Even when the family fortunes took an upturn, they seemed loath to spend any money on the house and by the time it came into the ownership of the

Above and right: Twisted columns in the North Drawing Room and diamond-pattern topiary at Ham House, left

National Trust in 1948, much restoration work was necessary.

Today the interior decoration is again sumptuous, with painted ceilings, gilded plasterwork and rich colours, and there is a particularly fine library. The garden is also being restored to its original design.

HAMMERWOOD PARK

Visitors to Hammerwood Park can enjoy their cream teas in the former kitchen below a replica of the Elgin Marbles.

There could be no more appropriate way of ending a tour of this extraordinary Greek Revival mansion, which was derelict when David Pinnegar took it over in 1982. It belonged previously to Led Zeppelin, the rock group, and before that had been clumsily converted into flats. The dining room has been left untouched to give an idea of the scale of the desolation while the Pinnegar family, who conduct the lively guided tours of their house, are tackling the restoration with heroic enthusiasm.

The house was built in 1792 as a grandiose hunting lodge. In spirit it is a temple to the Greek god Apollo, lord of hunting and the arts, and an inscription in Coade stone dates the house to the second year of the 642nd Olympiad. It was designed by Benjamin Latrobe, later famous for his work on the White House in Washington DC. There were subsequent modifications by S S Teulon, better known as an ecclesiastical architect. The house surveys, in Olympian calm, a beautiful view over rolling countryside to the south.

Inside the house, a collection of fine antiques complement the elegantly proportioned main rooms and the noble hall has been beautified with a delicious mural by two French artists, who spent three months balancing on scaffolding in Michelangelo style. At the same time, prams and Wellingtons scattered about the place are charming reminders that this is a family home as well as a showplace.

Built in 1792 as a Temple to Apollo, Hammerwood House has many fascinating features. The grounds are much admired for their spectacular arboretum, as well as rhododendrons, azaleas, acers and cornus

HAMPTON COURT Surrey

The landscaped flower gardens at Hampton Court Palace are a blaze of colour

In Tudor times, the quickest and easiest route to London from Hampton Court was by river. The great astronomical clock in the Clock Court enabled Henry VIII to determine the times of high and low tide at London Bridge.

Nearly 600 years of history are contained within this vast royal palace on the Thames. In the early 16th century the lease was acquired by Cardinal Wolsey, Henry VIII's chief minister, and he added most of the Tudor buildings that we see today. They included a complete range of apartments for the use of Henry VIII, Catherine of Aragon and Princess Mary. When the Cardinal fell from grace in the 1520s the palace was handed over to Henry as a placatory gesture and the King added the Great Hall, with its wonderful hammer-beam ceiling, and vast kitchens to cater for his 1,000-strong retinue. Later monarchs all left their mark, too.

There is so much to see at Hampton Court that six separate routes have been devised, each exploring a different theme: Henry VIII's magnificent state apartments; the Queen's apartments, built by Sir Christopher Wren for Queen Mary; the elegant Georgian rooms; the King's apartments, built by William III and restored following a dreadful fire in 1986; the Wolsey Rooms, the earliest of the Tudor Rooms which now house important Renaissance paintings; and the Tudor kitchens, which occupy over fifty rooms and are set up as if in preparation for a great Tudor banquet. Some 60 acres (24ha) of gardens include the famous maze and the Great Vine.

HEVER CASTLE Kent

3 miles (5km) south east of Edenbridge | Open selected days March to December | Tel: 01732 865224 | www.hevercastle.co.uk

Hever is not really a castle, but a double-moated manor house. There are four crucial periods in its building and family history – the 13th century, the mid-15th and 16th centuries and the early 1900s – and four famous figures dominate Hever's story. The first is the bewitching Anne Boleyn, second wife of King Henry VIII and the mother of Queen Elizabeth I. Hever Castle was her childhood home. She lived dangerously and died young when the executioner's sword severed her pretty, slender neck in the Tower of London.

The second figure is King Henry himself, who came to Hever to court her. The third is his fourth wife, the distinctly unbewitching Anne of Cleves, to whom he gave the estate. The fourth, 350 years later, is the American multi-millionaire William Waldorf Astor, who rescued Hever from gentle decline and, with admirable taste and judgement and a mountain of money, created the romantically beautiful house and grounds of today.

The oldest part of Hever is the sternly massive gatehouse, which was built in about 1270 and today houses some instruments of torture and punishment. There was a strong wall around the bailey, or yard, and the whole place was protected by a moat. Nothing else of much importance happened for two hundred years or so, until the appearance of the Bullens, or Boleyns.

The Bullens transformed Hever from a crude castle into a comfortable residence, built round a central courtyard. What is now the inner hall, with its rich Edwardian woodwork, was their Great Kitchen. There's a copy of the famous Holbein portrait of Henry VIII, with portraits of both Anne and Mary Boleyn, and the clock on the mantelpiece is a copy of the one that Henry gave Anne as

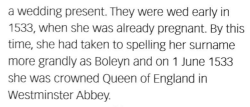

The childhood home of Anne Boleyn, double-moated Hever Castle (above) has a surprisingly cosy atmosphere (left)

a wedding present. They were wed early in 1533, when she was already pregnant. By this time, she had taken to spelling her surname more grandly as Boleyn and on 1 June 1533 she was crowned Queen of England in Westminster Abbey.

At Hever are touching mementos of Anne's short life, including embroidery that she worked. In the little bedroom that was hers as a girl are portraits of her and the prayer book that she carried with her to the block on Tower Green. In it she wrote, 'Remember me when you do pray, that hope doth lead from day to day, Anne Boleyn.'

As you proceed round the house, you have to keep mentally switching from the 16th century to the 20th and back. The drawing room, morning room and library are wonderfully luxurious Edwardian creations, but at the same time eminently liveable-in.

HIGHCLERE CASTLE Berkshire

Star of the ITV drama series *Downton Abbey* in autumn 2010, Highclere is approached through 6,000 acres (2,428ha) of rolling meadows and ancient cedars. And when, at last, the house heaves dramatically into view it doesn't disappoint. If it bears a strong resemblance to the Houses of Parliament, it is not surprising – Sir Charles Barry built Parliament and Highclere concurrently; the latter was completed in 1842.

The entrance hall continues the exterior Gothic theme with polychrome marble and a fan-vaulted roof. The beautifully carved pair of wyverns (winged dragons with two legs and a serpent's tail) represent the family crest. Period contrasts are a hallmark of Highclere, and the next room is a sumptuous Victorian library, also by Barry.

Between the drawing room and the smoking room is a curious set of pigeon-holes that were hidden for some sixty-seven years, the doors locked and barred by heavy furniture. When rediscovered, they were found to contain ancient artefacts from the 5th Earl's expeditions to Egypt.

The other passion of the 5th Earl was horse racing, and it was he who founded the now world-famous and renowned stud at

The delightful Monks' Garden at Highclere is just one of its highlights, as seen on ITV's 'Downton Abbey'

Highclere. The present Earl is Racing Manager to the Queen and the castle has an exhibition on the Highclere Stud.

The architectural tour de force of the house is undoubtedly its Saloon. This is a pure 'Cathedral Gothic' grand hall, with a splendid first-floor arcaded gallery and a soaring vaulted roof. Other highlights include the Stuart Revival dining room with a classic equestrian Charles I by Van Dyck, and outstanding gardens.

KENSINGTON PALACE London

Kensington Gardens, W8 | Open most days | Tel: 0844 482 7777 | www.KensingtonPalace@hrp.org.uk

Currently undergoing a £12 million transformation, this elegant palace is best known today as the erstwhile home of Diana, Princess of Wales.

In 1689, William III, who suffered badly from asthma, bought what was then called Nottingham House, the country home of the Earl of Nottingham. He employed Sir Christopher Wren to remodel it and moved the royal household from Whitehall to the cleaner country air of Kensington. The palace was enlarged and redecorated again for George I and was the principal private residence of the royal family until the death of George II. Queen Victoria was born here, and it was at Kensington Palace, in 1837, that she learned of her accession to the throne at the age of seventeen. The palace is now the London home of several members of the royal family, including Prince Charles and Prince and Princess Michael of Kent.

The state apartments, with rooms by Wren and William Kent, are furnished with pieces from the royal collection, and other rooms are sumptuously decorated in classical 18th-century style, with wonderful painted ceilings and fine works of art, including a large number of royal portraits. The palace is also the home of the Royal Ceremonial Dress Collection, which contains some of the magnificent costumes worn at Court from 1750 onwards, including dresses worn by Queen Victoria at all stages of her life.

The King's Staircase (below) is a grand reminder of past royal residents inside Kensington Palace (below left)

5 miles (8km) west of Abingdon | Opening times vary; check website before visiting | Tel: 01865 820259 | www.kingstonbagpuizehouse.org.uk

Miss Marlie Raphael bought Kingston Bagpuize House from Lord Ebury in 1939. When she died, in 1976, she was succeeded by her niece, Lady Grant, now Lady Tweedsmuir. Her father-in-law was the writer John Buchan, most famous for his action-packed adventure stories, such as *The Thirty Nine Steps*.

Mystery surrounds the origins of Kingston Bagpuize House. Some experts date it to about 1710, because it looks like the work of Wren and Gibbs. However, the family has found deeds showing that the house existed in 1670, and other suggested architects are Sir Roger Pratt, who built nearby Coleshill in 1652, and William Townesend.

The high-ceilinged rooms have Queen Anne fireplaces and a wealth of architectural detail; the furniture is mainly a mixture of French and English pieces from the 18th century. One of the most striking features of the house is the staircase and gallery, magnificently cantilevered so that the wall supports all the weight, leaving the entrance hall free of pillars. You can best appreciate the symmetrical design of the house from the saloon, which was originally the entrance hall, and from where the main ground-floor rooms can be seen. There are some interesting pictures, including one of Miss Raphael as a child.

The dining room, which was panelled in oak in 1728, contains a grandfather clock showing the phases of the moon. In the library is an intricately carved chimney piece in the style of Grinling Gibbons. The next room is a charming small morning room, which may once have been a bedroom. Its panelling was found in the stables by the indomitable Miss Raphael, who had it restored to its rightful place.

Upstairs there are five bedrooms. One of these, the Rose Room, was originally the Great Chamber, when it was larger by one

bay. Lady Tweedsmuir's bedroom was the original drawing room of the house. Look out for the Victorian doll's house on your way down the stairs. The late Miss Raphael's influence goes well beyond the house, for she also laid out the English garden, extending it beyond the mellow brick walls,

The staircase and gallery is one of Kingston Bagpuize House's most interesting architectural features

and creating a woodland garden and a large shrub border. There is also an early 18th-century gazebo built over an Elizabethan cockpit.

KNEBWORTH HOUSE Hertfordshire

2 miles (3km) south of Stevenage | Open selected afternoons March to September | Tel: 01438 812661 | www.knebworthhouse.com

Edward Bulwer, author of *The Last Days of Pompeii* and other successful works, inherited Knebworth from his mother, who was a Lytton, in 1843. Armed with a romantic disposition and plenty of money, he added Lytton to his surname and transformed the old Tudor manor house into the medieval fantasy of towers and turrets, battlements and machicolations, domelets and heraldic beasts that greets the astounded eye today.

Gothic horror films have been made here, and scenes for the remake of *The Big Sleep* with Robert Mitchum. Inside, however, is a charming old family home, warm with over five centuries of hospitality since Sir Robert Lytton built his house here in about 1500. His portrait is in the banqueting hall, as is a painting of the room by Sir Winston Churchill, who was often a guest. The door at one side allowed robust 18th-century drinkers to retire to the wine cellar and finish a bin in peace.

A vast portrait of Bulwer-Lytton as a young man hangs above the noble main staircase, which was created by his designer, the brilliant John Crace, and on the landing is a famous, melodramatic painting of him by Daniel Maclise. Crace designed the grand State Drawing Room with its Gothic furniture.

In one room there's a display relating to Lady Constance Lytton, the suffragette, who called herself Jane Wharton to avoid any special treatment because of her title when she was arrested. Sir Edwin Lutyens, who was married to her sister, Lady Emily, remodelled the Knebworth gardens. Following the death of the 2nd Earl in 1947 the estate passed to his daughter and her husband, Lord Cobbold, the distinguished banker, whose family have lived at Knebworth ever since.

Knebworth House, a medieval fantasy of towers and turrets, is popular as a film set

LOSELEY HOUSE Surrey

This beautiful Tudor mansion in its spreading park preserves both the mellowed stone of medieval Waverley Abbey and handsome panelling from Henry VIII's vanished Nonsuch Palace. Sir William More built his new manor house in the 1560s, since when it has descended to successive generations of the More and More-Molyneux families, and it has the atmosphere and the much-loved possessions of a cherished home.

Sir Christopher More bought the estate originally in Henry VII's time. The famous Sir Thomas More, executed by Henry VIII, was the stepson of Sir Christopher's sister and there is a portrait of him in the house. Sir Christopher's son, Sir William, was a devoted friend and servant of Elizabeth I. He was succeeded by Sir George, whose daughter Ann secretly married the poet John Donne when she was only seventeen; Sir George had his son-in-law put in prison for a year, but they were later reconciled. Elizabeth I and James I both visited Loseley on more than one occasion, and James I presented the portraits of himself and his queen that hang in the Great Hall.

The gilded ceiling in the drawing room is decorated with moorhens, mulberry trees and cockatrices – all family emblems – and the ornate chimneypiece, astonishingly, is carved from a single block of chalk. Queen Elizabeth I herself is believed to have worked the cushions on the two Tudor chairs.

The estate is well known for its herd of Jersey cows, which originally supplied the milk (and brand name) for Loseley dairy products, particularly the delicious ice cream. The house is often in demand as a film location.

The Great Hall (right) at Loseley House is hung with portraits of important historical figures including King James I and his queen, who visited here on more than one occasion

MICHELHAM PRIORY East Sussex

Michelham Priory is surrounded by one of the biggest moats in England, created in the 1380s for seclusion as much as defence, by diverting an arm of the River Cuckmere.

The Priory of the Holy Trinity was founded in 1229 by a prominent local family. It was staffed by canons of the Augustinian Order – not monks exactly, but priests living together here and serving the local parishes. After the Priory closed, in 1537, the house was turned into a country gentleman's residence, principally by Herbert Pelharn, a Sussex ironmaster who bought the property some fifty years later. In 1601 it was sold to the wealthy Sackville family of Knole in Sevenoaks, who became Earls and later Dukes of Dorset, though they never took up residence at Michelham.

The Sackville era ended in 1891, when Michelham was sold to James Gwynne, who commenced a programme of restoration. Work on the priory continued from the 1920s by the Beresford-Wright family (whose money came from Wright's Coal Tar Soap). Canadian troops were billeted here in the 1940s and a plan for the ill-fated Dieppe Raid of 1942 can still be seen, outlined on one of the gatehouse walls.

Since 1959, Michelham has belonged to the Sussex Archaeological Society, and the

Protected from intruders by one of the largest moats in England, Michelham Priory is charmingly secluded

tapestries, furniture, samplers and other items on show in the Priory come from its collections. They include a marvellous assemblage of musical instruments from the Alice Schulmann Frank Collection (Alice was the cousin of Anne Frank, of Diary fame). These are on display in the Music Room, with its beautiful walnut panelling and modern stained-glass windows.

On the south lawn is a recreation of a monastic physic garden, containing nearly 100 different types of medicinal plants.

NETHER WINCHENDON HOUSE Bucks

5 miles (8km) east of Thame, Junc 6 M40 | **Open most afternoons April to May and August BH** | **Tel: 01844 290101** | **www.netherwinchendonhouse.com**

A medieval house? Parts of it are, with Tudor alterations, and the eye-catching battlemented screen wall of three arches into the courtyard is late 18th-century Gothic. Sir Scrope Bernard redesigned the original medieval and Tudor exterior and clad the older timber-framed buildings in stone: a romantic 18th-century transformation.

Some of the most interesting parts of the house date from the early 16th century, when it was owned by the Abbey of Notley, but let to one of Henry VIII's top civil servants, Sir John Daunce. He added a parlour (now the drawing room), and his initials, portrait, rebus and coat-of-arms feature in the superbly carved Renaissance oak frieze.

The house was sold in 1559 to a London merchant, William Goodwin, and since then has descended by inheritance to the present owner. Goodwin's daughter married into a long-established Buckinghamshire family, the Tyringhams. Later the house went to their cousins, the Bernards, then the Spencers, whose family still live there. The first Bernard at Nether Winchendon was Sir Francis, last British Governor of New Jersey and Massachusetts, who is remembered in the names of four US towns: Bernard, Bernardston, Bernardsville and Winchendon. Sir Francis's third son, Thomas, was a notable social reformer and philanthropist.

The manorial court met in the panelled 13th-century Great Hall, presided over by the Lord of the Manor, and court rolls on display date back to 1530. Family portraits adorn the walls, including one of Thomas Tyringham, born in 1559, the first of the family to be born and bred here. Splendid lawns run from the south front down to the River Thame.

Nether Winchendon House has passed by family descent for 400 years and is still a family home

OSBORNE HOUSE
Isle of Wight

Queen Victoria and Prince Albert, dissatisfied with the turmoil of life at Court, decided to seek a peaceful holiday retreat large and private enough for their needs. Recalling happy childhood holidays, Victoria turned her attention to the Isle of Wight and in 1844 the royal couple rented Osborne House for a year's trial period. Though the original house proved too small, its situation on rising ground overlooking the Solent delighted the royal couple and they bought the house and its 1,000 acres (405ha) of land in 1845.

Prince Albert compared the view from Osborne to the Bay of Naples, and when he and his builder, Thomas Cubitt, drew up plans for a new house it took the form of a Neapolitan villa, with Italianate campaniles and a loggia. The Prince, as keen on science and industry as he was on architecture, employed innovative construction methods, including the use of cast-iron beams.

Outside, Albert created mock Renaissance terraces, with statues and a fountain, reaching down to the sea where they had a private beach, and planted acres of trees on the surrounding estate. He also imported a Swiss chalet as a play house for the royal children, but it had an educational purpose too – the boys were taught carpentry, the princesses learned cooking, and each of the children had a garden plot to tend. When Prince Albert died from typhoid in 1861, the heartbroken Queen issued instructions that nothing at Osborne should be changed so that it would remain as a memorial to the man who had created it.

Hardly anything has changed here since Queen Victoria died either, and there are many of her personal possessions, including her own and Prince Albert's paintings and gifts among the grand works of art and statues which adorn the state rooms.

Below and right: The Pavilion and Drawing Room at Osborne House, in the care of English Heritage

OSTERLEY Middlesex

The area between Heathrow Airport and Chiswick hardly seems a likely location for a splendid mansion set in 140 acres (56ha) of parkland, but this is where you will find Osterley Park, one of the last surviving country estates in London.

The original red-brick Tudor house dates back to 1575, when it was built for Sir Thomas Gresham, founder of the Royal Exchange, but it is actually known today as one of the most complete examples of the work of Robert Adam. Between 1760 and 1780 Adam transformed the house into a superb Neoclassical villa, with the intricate plasterwork for which he was famous. By this time, Osterley was owned by Robert Child, a wealthy London banker.

The house is entered by a huge double portico, built between the two towers of the original building, and this leads into a magnificent entrance hall with Roman statues and stucco panels. The state apartments include an ornately decorated four-poster bed, an ante-room with Gobelin tapestries and a dressing room decorated in the Etruscan style, its walls ornamented with classical figures and urns.

The Long Gallery, which occupies the entire length of the west front, was designed to house the Childs' picture collection. The furniture in the gallery was designed by John Linnell, an associate of Robert Adam. As well as a collection of 17th- and 18th-century Venetian art, it houses two Chinese imperial junks, a pair of Chinese pagodas, and 18th-century Oriental porcelain.

Adam's involvement at Osterley did not stop at the house: he also built the semi-circular garden house, with stucco medallions of festive figures and Ionic pilasters, within the landscaped grounds.

East front with 'transparent' portico (top), Etruscan Dressing Room (right) and the entrance hall (left)

PALACE HOUSE, BEAULIEU Hampshire

7 miles (11km) south east of Lyndhurst | Open every day except Christmas Day | Tel: 01590 612345 | www.beaulieu.co.uk

Beaulieu is an unashamedly modern tourist attraction with a state-of-the-art museum, an overhead monorail and other Disney-style trappings. Yet the estate dates back to 1204, when a Cistercian Abbey was founded here by King John. It was, until then, the site of a royal hunting lodge named Bellus Locus Regis – 'the beautiful place of the king'. The Cistercians, a French order, rechristened it 'beau lieu' ('beautiful place'), pronouncing it 'bewley' just as it is today.

The Abbey was dissolved in 1538 by Henry VIII and the estate sold to Sir Thomas Wriothsley. Most of the buildings were demolished, but Wriothsley turned the Great Gatehouse into a manor house-cum-hunting lodge, which is the basis of the present house. The Wriothsley name continued until 1667, when Elizabeth Wriothsley inherited Beaulieu and married into the Montagu family. After just one generation, however, the 2nd Duke of Montagu died without a male heir and the famous Scott family (the Dukes of Buccleuch) took over the Beaulieu estate.

During the 18th century the Great Gatehouse – by then known as Palace House – had been fortified against the threat of a French invasion, but when Lord Henry Scott moved into Beaulieu in 1867 he found it little changed since monastic times and he commissioned Sir Arthur Blomfield to redesign it in Victorian-Gothic style.

The National Motor Museum has over 300 vehicles, ranging from an 1896 Peugeot to a 2004 Ferrari Enzo, alongside world record-breakers like the legendary *Bluebird*.

Concentrating on the Victorian period, Palace House is at the heart of the many tourist attractions at Beaulieu

PARHAM PARK West Sussex

On 28 January 1577, 'at about ten of the clock in the forenoon', the foundation stone of the new house at Parham was formally laid by a boy of two-and-a-half, Thomas Palmer. The Palmers bought Parham in 1540 after the Dissolution of the Monasteries. An Elizabethan creation in greyish brown stone, the house is today a treasure trove of rare needlework, paintings, furniture, tapestries, china and oriental carpets.

The principal Elizabethan room is the Great Hall, light and airy with its tall windows, a double cube with a moulded ceiling and carved oak screen, where the whole household ate together. There is an old tradition that Elizabeth I dined here in 1593. The hall contains a portrait of James I's eldest son which, when cleaned in 1985, revealed an entirely unsuspected allegorical picture.

The Great Parlour, charmingly panelled, was the family's private sitting room in the 16th century, while the elegant Saloon was redecorated in cream and gold in about 1790.

Thomas Palmer, the little boy who laid the foundation stone, served at sea under Sir Francis Drake and sold Parham in 1601 to Thomas Bysshop, who obtained a baronetcy from James I and whose descendants lived

The magnificent Long Gallery affords stunning views over the Deer Park to the South Downs beyond

here for three centuries. In 1922 Parham was sold to the Honourable Clive Pearson, son of the 1st Viscount Cowdray, and he and his wife devoted themselves to restoring and bringing life back to the house. It was Mrs Pearson and her mother, Lady Brabourne, who assembled Parham's wonderful collection of embroidery and tapestry from the 17th-century and later, which is probably the best in the country. Their own work can also be seen in the house.

PENSHURST PLACE Kent

The round pond in the Italian Garden at Penshurst Place and Gardens

The original part of Penshurst Place was built between 1340 and 1345 for Sir John de Pulteney, and although it has been extended and modified by successive owners its magnificent baron's hall remains superbly preserved. This was the heart of the medieval house, where the entire household lived and congregated for meals beneath the wonderful chestnut-beamed roof. Its central fireplace is still evident today, and it is renowned as the oldest and finest example of a medieval hall in the country.

Penshurst was closely connected with royalty, belonging at one time to Henry IV's third son, and later to Henry VIII. His son, Edward VI, gave the property to Sir William Sidney in 1552 and it is still the Sidney family home. A great variety of architectural styles are incorporated in the building we see today, though its battlemented exterior presents a unified face, and its series of interesting rooms provides a splendid backdrop for the superb furniture, crystal chandeliers, tapestries and works of art. There are family portraits everywhere, including one of that famous ancestor, Sir Philip Sidney, the great Elizabethan soldier, courtier and poet. A tremendous amount of restoration work has been carried out since World War II, when Penshurst was damaged by flying bombs, and it is as much a monument to the most recent generations of Sidneys as to its great figures of the past.

POLESDEN LACEY Surrey

3 miles (5km) north west of Dorking | Open selected days March to October | Tel: 01372 458203 | **www.nationaltrust.org.uk**

Polesden Lacey really came into its own during the Edwardian era, when the estate belonged to the Honourable Ronald Greville and his wife. Until the outbreak of World War II the house was alive with high society gatherings, presided over by the vivacious Mrs Greville. The daughter of the Right Hon. William McEwan, one-time Member of Parliament and founder of the McEwan brewery, Mrs Greville was a charming but determined lady with high social ambitions. Through her husband's connections she found her way into the Marlborough House circle of Edward VII. After her husband died in 1908, she capitalized on those introductions until she was a much sought-after hostess, entertaining the King and his friends on a lavish scale at Polesden Lacey. The Duke and Duchess of York (later George VI and Queen Elizabeth) spent part of their honeymoon here. The visitors' books, menus, photographs and newspaper cuttings that survive here are, perhaps, the most telling reminders of the high life they all enjoyed.

'Ronnie' Greville's enormous strength of character still permeates Polesden Lacey today, and her fine collections of paintings, tapestries, porcelain and other works of art furnish the house in handsome style. On her death in 1942 she bequeathed the house to the National Trust as a memorial to her father. She is buried in the grounds.

The interior of the house consists of a series of fascinating rooms ranged around a central courtyard. The entrance hall, two storeys high, is both welcoming and impressive. The dining room, scene of Mrs Greville's sumptuous dinner parties, has some beautiful silver and porcelain, and the drawing room has carved and gilt panelling that may have come from an Italian palace.

A portrait of the vivacious Mrs Greville, painted in 1891 by Emile-Augustus Carolus-Duran

QUEX PARK Kent

Major Percy Powell-Cotton, who inherited the family estate of Quex Park in 1894, was a formidable naturalist, hunter, explorer and collector who loved 'to wander in distant lands'. He wandered to some effect, making twenty-eight expeditions to Africa and Asia, and shooting hundreds of animals. Bringing his specimens back home, he had them stuffed by the London taxidermy firm of Rowland Hill, the masters of the craft, and displayed in dioramas of their natural

Home of the Powell-Cotton Museum, Quex Park houses weaponry and natural history artefacts

habitats. In one of them is the lion that savaged him, almost fatally, in Africa in 1905. The jacket that the lion tore to bits can still be seen in the museum.

Powell-Cotton pioneered this type of display and the house at Birchington became home to more and more of his exotic exhibits, which started in the billiard room, colonized the house from there and spilled over into a specially built pavilion outside. The major opened his museum to the public in 1921. By the time he died in 1940, aged seventy-four, there were 500 animal specimens as well as thousands more

objects gathered on his travels – one of the finest African collections ever put together – an enormous assemblage of cannon and firearms, and a unique collection of Chinese imperial porcelain. The collections are now in a purpose-built museum next to the house, where the Powell-Cotton family still live.

The curious name Quex comes from the Quek family, which owned the estate during the 15th century. Today, as well as the dioramas and exhibits, many of the rooms in Quex House are still much as they were in Major Powell-Cotton's time, delightfully furnished in the Edwardian manner.

ST MARY'S HOUSE West Sussex

This haunting and venerable building – the finest example of Sussex half-timbering of its time – began life in 1470 as a galleried inn, kept by monks for the sustenance of pilgrims on the southern road to Canterbury. Besides its huge black interior beams, it has a unique 'shutting window' from that time. After the Dissolution of the Monasteries, St Mary's was turned into a private house and in the 16th century it belonged to Lord Calthorpe, who was Queen Elizabeth I's cousin. She came to visit him and the beautiful Painted Room was specially prepared for her, with superb trompe-l'oeil pine panelling. A later visitor was the young Charles II, who waited anxiously in the house on his way to escape across the Channel to France after the Battle of Worcester in 1651.

In the 1890s the house was bought by the Honourable Algernon Bourke, a son of the Earl of Mayo, owner of White's in London and a notable wit and *bon viveur*, who added the beautiful music room where concerts are again held today. Alfred Musgrave bought the house in 1903 and the Sherlock Holmes story of *The Musgrave Ritual* is set here, mentioning the two huge trees that stood in the garden until the 1980s.

In the 1940s St Mary's was only just saved from a developer who would have knocked it flat. In 1984 it was bought by Peter Thorogood, and the Thorogood and Linton families have been busy since, sensitively and stylishly restoring it.

An unexpected bonus for today's visitor is Peter Thorogood's unrivalled collection of material related to Thomas Hood, the 19th-century humorous writer, while outside the charming garden has many delightful examples of topiary and is said to be stalked by spectral monks.

The drawing room at St Mary's House is filled with interesting and diverse objects

SOUTHSIDE HOUSE London

South side of Wimbledon Common | Open selected afternoons from Easter until the end of September | Tel: 020 8946 7643 | **www.southsidehouse.com**

The owner of Southside House for many years was Mrs Hilda Munthe who, in 1907, married the Swedish doctor and philanthropist Axel Munthe, best known as the author of *The Story of San Michele*.

Parts of the book were written in the garden at Southside, where the youthful Lord Byron had liked to sit years before. Mrs Munthe, a beauty who, as a girl of sixteen, had declined a proposal from King Alexander of Serbia, was originally Hilda Pennington Mellor, a descendant of Robert Pennington. He retreated here in the 17th century from a plague-ridden London after the loss of his small son, converting what was a farmhouse into this grand house.

The property passed through a succession of descendants, including John Pennington, something of a Scarlet Pimpernel during the French Revolution, helping aristocrats to escape the mob. A necklace, strung from pearls that fell from Marie Antoinette's dress when she was guillotined, is still kept in the house. The house was restored after the war and there are family portraits and pictures by Van Dyck, Hogarth, Reynolds, Gainsborough and Burne-Jones. There are personal belongings of Anne Boleyn, distantly related by her sister's marriage, paintings by Viking Munthe, son of Axel and Hilda, and many other family treasures.

The elegant dining room (below left) and the grand staircase (below) at Southside House

SQUERRYES COURT Kent

This mellow red-brick manor house is in the William and Mary style, although it dates from Charles I's reign. In the 18th century it was owned by the Villiers family, Earls of Jersey. Meanwhile, a Yorkshireman named Sir Patience Warde made a fortune in London and became Lord Mayor in 1680, just as Squerryes was about to be built. The two strands came together in 1731, when the 3rd Earl of Jersey sold Squerryes to his friend John Warde, Sir Patience's great-nephew. The Wardes have lived there ever since and the house is a delightful monument to the family.

There is also a strong connection with General Wolfe, the 18th-century soldier who grew up at Quebec House nearby. A monument in the garden marks the spot where he was given his first commission and a room in the house is devoted to his memory. Benjamin West's portrait of him as a boy was commissioned by George Warde. In a glass case is Wolfe's mother's recipe for a

Jane Austen's 'Emma' was filmed at Squerryes for the BBC television production in 2009

medicine for consumption, involving ground snail-shells and earthworms freshly sliced with herbs simmered in milk.

The successive generations of Wardes are commemorated by a fine array of family portraits and there are pictures in the house by Van Dyck, Ruysdael, Stubbs and Opie, and a giant portrait of Philip II of Spain.

STANDEN West Sussex

2 miles (3km) south of East Grinstead | Open selected days February to December | Tel: 01342 323029 | www.nationaltrust.org.uk

Designed by the architect Philip Webb (1831-1915), this delightful house was built between 1891 and 1894 for a London solicitor, James Beale, and his family, and has become a showpiece of the 19th-century Arts and Crafts movement. Webb, along with William Morris (1834–1896), was a leading light of the movement, whose main principles concerned the promotion of genuine craftsmanship as opposed to the mass-production techniques so favoured by the Victorian age. Generally the architect would specify not only the building design but also the interior fittings and furniture, and accordingly Standen is furnished with some beautifully preserved William Morris wallpapers and fabrics. His designs here include the famous Sunflower, Peacock, Trellis and Larkspur motifs.

The furniture in the house was also custom-made and includes contemporary brass beds from Heal's, furniture from the Morris company and ceramics by William de Morgan – another big name of the Arts and Crafts period. Webb himself designed some of the furniture, as well as details such as the fire grates, the electric light fittings and the finger-plates for the doors.

Standen is a rambling house that looks for all the world as if it had developed over many centuries rather than having been completed in a relatively short space of time, and this is due to Webb's use of the vernacular style and traditional building materials. He extended the same principles to the gardens, using local building materials and natural colour schemes for his plantings.

Top: The dining room side table is thought to have been designed by Rathbone, while the silver-plated muffin dish was designed by Ashbee, c.1900

Most of the furniture in the drawing room (left) is by William Morris. The embroidered hangings in the bedroom (right) date from 1896

STANSTED PARK West Sussex

The Lumley family built Stansted House on its present site in 1688, at about the same time as nearby Uppark and using the same architect, William Talman. That house was altered in the 18th century by James Wyatt, but caught fire in 1900, resulting in the present house being partly an Edwardian rebuilding by Sir Reginald Blomfield and partly Georgian with later additions. The original Stansted was a hunting lodge, shattered by Parliamentary cannon in the Civil War and now incorporated into the Regency Gothic chapel. This is probably the only church in Britain to display the Ten Commandments in Hebrew: Lewis Way, Stansted's owner in the early 19th century, aimed to persuade the local Jews to convert to Christianity.

Stansted's spacious interiors provide a worthy setting for the splendid furniture, paintings and other works of art belonging to the Bessborough family. Indeed, the Bessboroughs bought the property to house their historic and valuable collection of paintings after fire destroyed their house in Kilkenny in the Republic of Ireland. The Blue Drawing Room, still lined with its original blue silk, contains four large Arcadian landscapes by the Dutch artist, Dalens, and furniture brought by the 10th Earl of Bessborough's mother, who was French.

By contrast, the music room has mainly modern family paintings, but also William and Mary and Queen Anne chairs and an 18th-century square piano. The main dining room evokes wonder and admiration with its Chinese famille-rose dinner service, Georgian silver and Waterford crystal. The old kitchen contains such items as a teak sink and a butter cupboard, once wheeled nightly into cold storage. There is also a small but well-equipped theatre built in 1985.

The fabulously decorated chancel inside Stansted Park's Regency Gothic chapel

STONOR PARK Oxfordshire

5 miles (8km) north of Henley-on-Thames | Open selected afternoons April to September | Tel: 01491 638587 | **www.stonor.com**

Stonor evolved over many centuries, but at its core is a group of medieval flint, chalk and clunch buildings. The oldest, dating from about 1190, is the Old Hall, which retains the original arches. A buttery (now a study), a solar (now the library) and the chapel were added between 1280 and 1341 and over the next two centuries, timber and flint additions were built. When Sir Walter Stonor took over the estate in 1534, he linked the buildings together to create a formal E-shaped Tudor house with a gabled brick facade.

These changes were financed by a fortune made from wool and sheep, and the acquisition of land by marriage. However, interest in home improvement lessened after the Reformation, when this staunchly Catholic family was heavily fined and penalized throughout many years of Catholic repression. The family sheltered priests on the run, most notably Edmund Campion, who supervised the printing of his *Decem Rationes* (Ten Reasons for Being a Catholic) in 1581 from a room behind the chimney in the roof. Stonor became a national centre for Catholicism, and indeed its chapel is one of only three in England where Mass has been continuously celebrated to this day.

In the 1750s, architect John Aitkins removed the Tudor forecourt, wall, gateway and lodges, to introduce fashionable Georgian features such as heavy cornice of the roof. Under the high, 16th-century barrel-vaulted ceiling of the library is a major collection of Catholic books, many illegally printed or imported during the Recusancy.

Surrounded by beech woods, Stonor is on the site of a prehistoric stone circle, which has been recreated in the grounds.

Stonor Park is delightfully set in beech woods in the rolling Oxfordshire countryside

STOWE HOUSE & GARDENS

Bucks

🐓 **2 miles (3km) north west of Buckingham** | **Open selected afternoons throughout the year** | **Tel: 01280 818166** | **www.nationaltrust.org.uk**

Stowe House and Gardens are from an era when men of wealth and power celebrated by ostentatiously pursuing the latest architectural and artistic fashions. The Temple family supported Parliament in the Civil War and became steadfast adherents of the Whig cause. They were against the Stuarts and absolutism, and in favour of the independence and power of the landowning aristocracy. All of this was expressed in lavish display by Sir Richard Temple (1675–1749). An outspoken soldier with political ambitions, he was probably the richest man in England when he set about turning Stowe from a

country house into a palace. And the grand design for this celebration of power starts two miles away in Buckingham, where the great vista of the approach to Stowe begins. Visiting VIPs were driven along this highway for a mile, enjoying views of the porticoed south front with its curving colonnaded wings, then led away through trees to the carriage entrance on the north side.

The Temple family went from strength to strength, becoming Earls, then Marquesses, and finally Dukes of Buckingham. They employed a whole string of celebrated architects, including Vanbrugh, Kent, Gibbs,

The Palladian Bridge (above) and the Gothic Temple and Octagon Lake (right), designed by James Gibbs in 1731

Adam and Soane, to improve the house, and continued to develop its landscape setting. They also applied their wealth and taste to furnishing and adorning its interiors; the state rooms of the piano nobile or ceremonial first floor are particularly outstanding.

The wonderful landscaped gardens were put in the care of the National Trust (with an endowment) in 1989, in order that they could restore the forty listed monuments and temples and increase access for the public.

SYON HOUSE Middlesex

Off Twickenham Road, Brentford, via Park Road | Open selected days spring to autumn | Tel: 020 8560 0882 | **www.syonpark.co.uk**

Syon was the country refuge of the Dukes of Northumberland, descendants of the formidable Percy dynasty. The estate was named after Mount Zion in the Holy Land by the nuns who owned it at the end of the Middle Ages. In 1547 Lord Protector Somerset began to build the house that stands there today (though it has been greatly altered), and two mulberry trees he planted in the grounds still bear fruit.

Lady Jane Grey was fatally offered the crown at Syon, which came to the Northumberlands under Queen Elizabeth and James I. In the 18th century the 1st Duke of Northumberland found the place 'ruinous and inconvenient'. To remedy this, 'Capability' Brown was called in to work his magic on the grounds and Robert Adam to design the state rooms, which are the glory of the house.

During World War II sixty-nine bombs fell on Syon, but the great mansion somehow survived. The interiors are breathtaking; the entrance hall may well be the finest in all England. Cool, quiet, soothing in grey, white and blue, it is staffed by statues of noble Romans in marble. Steps lead up to a second, contrasting hall, which is ablaze with lifesize gilded statues on marble pillars in black and swirling shades of grey. You proceed through Corinthian pillars into the delectable dining room, 66 feet (20m) long and a splendour of cream and gold. The Three Graces pose sweetly in a roundel over the chimneypiece and above them, in a graceful compliment, is a portrait head of Northumberland's duchess.

Outside, as well as the beautiful grounds, are an art centre, a butterfly house, a miniature steam railway, a soaring glasshouse, which was a forerunner of Crystal Palace, and one of the best garden centres in the south of England.

Elegant statuary and marble pillars decorate the Great Hall at Syon House

THE VYNE Hampshire

4 miles (6km) north of Basingstoke | Open selected days March to September | Tel: 01256 883858 | www.nationaltrust.org.uk

The Vyne was built at the beginning of the 16th century by William Sandys, a loyal and discreet member of Henry VIII's court who rose to become Lord Chamberlain and entertained the King on several occasions at his Hampshire home. Elizabeth I was also a visitor, but during the Civil War it was Parliamentarians rather than Royalists who assembled there. That struggle considerably reduced the Sandys fortune, so that the 6th Lord Sandys found it necessary to sell the house and retire to his other home – Mottisfont Abbey, near Romsey.

The new owner was Chaloner Chute, a prosperous barrister with a reputation as an unbiased and just advocate, who had managed to avoid politics during the Civil War, but later became a Member of Parliament and Speaker of the House. He made various improvements to The Vyne before his death in 1659. His grandson, Edward, was responsible for the collection of fine Queen Anne furniture and Soho tapestries that can now be seen in the house.

Another Chute to leave his mark on the house was Edward's son, John, who, after an initial reluctance to inherit The Vyne at all, designed for it a spectacular classical-style staircase hall. On the ground floor of the house, the Stone Gallery occupies the whole of the west wing and contains a series of busts and statues. From here, rooms stretch along the north side of the house, including the 'further' drawing room with its delicate plaster ceiling, the ante-room, with its fine collection of china and porcelain, and the 'large' drawing room, where a carved fireplace is painted to resemble stone. The dining room has Elizabethan wood panelling and a charming pair of paintings by Sebastian Pether entitled *Sunrise and Moonlight*.

The Vyne was built in the early 16th century for Lord Sandys, Henry VIII's Lord Chamberlain

Successive generations of Dashwoods have been trying to live down the exploits of the second Sir Francis, who gained notoriety as a member of the Hell Fire Club. It is carefully pointed out these days that he was also Postmaster General from 1766 to 1781, and was also responsible for the transformation of West Wycombe House (built by his predecessor), continuing to make improvements until his death in 1781.

West Wycombe is much as the second Sir Francis left it, and is acknowledged as an important monument to neoclassicism. Behind the facades, which include a double colonnade on the south front and a splendid Ionic portico on the west, are a series of rooms that continue the classical theme. The hall and staircase have been likened to a Roman atrium, the painted ceiling of the saloon represents the Council of the Gods, and that in the Blue Drawing Room – formerly the dining room – depicts the Triumph of Bacchus and Ariadne.

Opening on to the east portico is the Music Room, the largest room in the house, whose frescoed ceiling depicting the 'Banquet of the Gods' was copied from the Villa Farnesina in Rome. The Saloon, in the centre of the north front, contains many marble statuettes, including one of the four

West Wycombe House was transformed into this classical mansion in the 18th century

seasons. Much of the decoration is very rare, and is complemented with fine paintings and tapestries. The Tapestry Room, for example, contains tapestries given to the 1st Duke of Marlborough – a distant relative of the Dashwoods – to mark his victories in the War of Spanish Succession (1701–14).

The mansion is set in extensive landscaped grounds containing many follies and temples. These include the Temple of Music set on an island in the swan-shaped lake and used as a theatre.

WOBURN ABBEY Bedfordshire

8 miles (13km) north west of Dunstable | Open daily spring to autumn | Tel: 01525 290333 | www.woburn.co.uk

Woburn Abbey shows few outward signs of having once been a religious foundation. It is an 18th-century English nobleman's palace built on the foundations of a Cistercian abbey – a palace adorned with treasures assembled by a dozen generations of a family with both taste and money. Its grand state apartments, including the State Saloon and State Dining Room, are palatial both in scale and the magnificence of their decor. These, and the more comfortably scaled family rooms, house an astoundingly rich art collection – for instance, a room full of views of Venice by Canaletto, commissioned by the 4th Duke; another hung with family portraits by Sir Joshua Reynolds.

Perhaps the most serenely beautiful room in this south (family) wing is the library. In effect, it comprises three rooms, divided by screen walls with fluted Corinthian columns, and is lined with recessed bookshelves of finely bound volumes (predominantly on the subject of natural history), which beautifully complement the decorative plasterwork above. Hanging over the bookcases is a series of remarkable portraits, including a Rembrandt self-portrait and his wonderful study, *The Old Rabbi*.

Woburn Abbey is now the venue for all kinds of commercial events, from the East Midlands Doll Fair to rallies of historic vehicles. It is lived in and managed by the heir to the dukedom, the Marquis of Tavistock, and his wife and family. They endeavour to provide a range of attractions that appeals to all age groups.

Queen Victoria's bedroom. The Queen slept in this bed when she visited in 1841

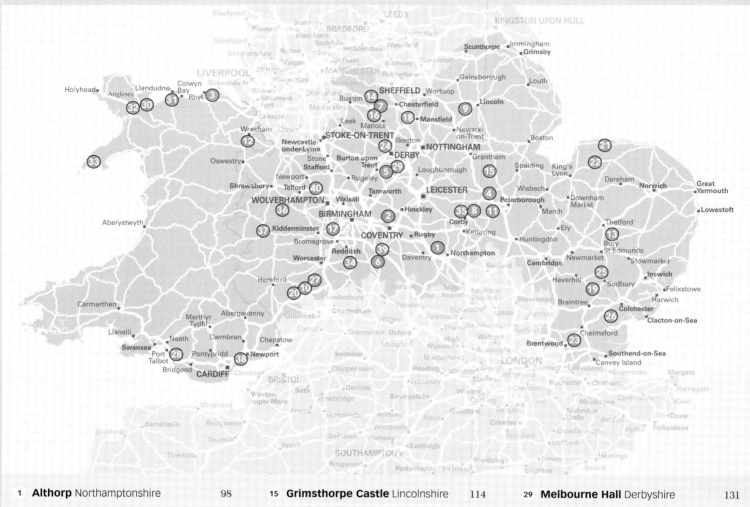

1	**Althorp** Northamptonshire	98
2	**Arbury Hall** Warwickshire	99
3	**Bodrhyddan Hall** Denbighshire	100
4	**Burghley House** Lincolnshire	101
5	**Calke Abbey** Derbyshire	102
6	**Charlecote Park** Warwickshire	103
7	**Chatsworth** Derbyshire	104
8	**Deene Park** Northamptonshire	106
9	**Doddington Hall** Lincolnshire	107
10	**Eastnor Castle** Herefordshire	108
11	**Elton Hall** Cambridgeshire	109
12	**Erddig** Wrexham	110
13	**Euston Hall** Norfolk	112
14	**Eyam Hall** Derbyshire	113
15	**Grimsthorpe Castle** Lincolnshire	114
16	**Haddon Hall** Derbyshire	115
17	**Hagley Hall** West Midlands	116
18	**Hardwick Hall** Derbyshire	117
19	**Hedingham Castle** Essex	119
20	**Hellens** Herefordshire	120
21	**Holkham Hall** Norfolk	122
22	**Houghton Hall** Norfolk	123
23	**Ingatestone Hall** Essex	124
24	**Kedleston Hall** Derbyshire	125
25	**Kentwell Hall** Suffolk	127
26	**Layer Marney Tower** Essex	128
27	**Little Malvern Court** Worcestershire	129
28	**Margam Country Park** Neath	130
29	**Melbourne Hall** Derbyshire	131
30	**Penrhyn Castle** Gwynedd	132
31	**Plas Mawr** Conwy	135
32	**Plas Newydd** Gwynedd	136
33	**Plas yn Rhiw** Gwynedd	137
34	**Ragley Hall** Warwickshire	138
35	**Rockingham Castle** Leicestershire	139
36	**Shipton Hall** Shropshire	140
37	**Stokesay Court** Shropshire	141
38	**Tredegar House** Newport	142
39	**Warwick Castle** Warwickshire	144
40	**Weston Park** Shropshire	145

CENTRAL ENGLAND, EAST ANGLIA, WALES & THE MARCHES

The great houses of Central England can teach important lessons in architectural styles: from the mighty medieval fortifications of Warwick Castle, to the moated Tudor mellowness of Kentwell Hall, and the Cecils' grandeur at Burghley House, expressed in a riot of Jacobean domes and pinnacles. Two of the grandest Palladian palaces in the country – Houghton Hall and Holkham Hall – vie for supremacy in Norfolk, while Somerleyton Hall embodies Victorian lavishness. Further west, in Wales and the Marches, are houses rejoicing in long histories and curious juxtapositions – like the Egyptian mummy in Bodrhyddan Hall. There is drama in the Malvern Hills, where you can imagine Sir Ivanhoe jousting at Eastnor Castle, a splendid fake Norman fortress of 1812; and Hellen's, in Much Marcle, is still home to descendants of the great Marcher warlords, the Mortimers. Times of peace brought elegance as the Morgans held sway from Tredegar House, with its graceful 17th-century brick, while Weston Park, another grand brick edifice, brims over with Old Master paintings.

ALTHORP Northamptonshire

In 1981, the 8th Earl Spencer, owner of Althorp, escorted his daughter up the aisle of St Paul's Cathedral, where she married Charles, the Prince of Wales. Princess Diana was not the first in her family to become a figure of national importance, however. The wealthy Robert, 2nd Earl of Sunderland, was a diplomat for James I; his grandson fought for the Royalists in the Civil War. Later Spencers included a First Lord of the Admiralty and a Chancellor of the Exchequer.

Sir John Spencer bought Althorp in the early 16th century. It is likely that the house remained unaltered until the mid-17th century, when the widow of the 1st Earl of Sunderland roofed the courtyard over and added an imposing staircase to form what is known today as the Saloon.

The flamboyant 2nd Earl of Sunderland decided that the dignified red-brick house did not properly reflect his position at Court and set about altering it. He added Corinthian columns and a balustrade to the front of the house, drained the moat, and turned the Elizabethan Great Hall into a Long Gallery. Thirty years after the 2nd Earl's death, the splendid Italianate stable block was built and remains one of the best architectural features of Althorp.

The death of Diana, Princess of Wales, on 31 August 1997 prompted an unprecedented outpouring of grief worldwide. Diana was buried on an island in the centre of the Round Oval lake at Althorp. Visitors can walk the parameter of the lake, where there is a temple dedicated to Diana's memory. In the stable block, an award-winning exhibition entitled 'Diana: A Celebration' includes audio-visual displays, childhood letters and school reports and, of course, the famous wedding dress by David and Elizabeth Emanuel.

Opulent paintings and furnishings inside the childhood home of Princess Diana at Althorp

ARBURY HALL Warwickshire

2½ miles (4km) south of Nuneaton | Open Bank Holiday weekends; groups by appointment | Tel: 02476 382804 | **www.arburyestate.co.uk**

On 22 November 1819, Mary Ann Evans was born at South Farm on the Arbury Estate. Under her pen name of George Eliot, she became one of the great English novelists, and Arbury Hall and its surroundings were among her earliest inspirations. Arbury features as Cheverel Manor in her *Scenes of Clerical Life*, in which she describes how the house grew 'from ugliness into beauty' under the direction of Sir Christopher Cheverel. In real life, this was Sir Roger Newdigate, who is responsible for how Arbury looks today.

Arbury Hall was originally an Elizabethan courtyard house, to which the handsome, symmetrical, classical stable block to the north west was added in the 1670s. Its main decorative feature is the porch, designed by Sir Christopher Wren. From 1748 until his death in 1806, Sir Roger transformed Arbury Hall into an outstanding work of the Gothic Revival. The light, exuberant style of the rebuilding was a reaction against the strict classicism that had come to cominate English architecture.

Entry to the house is through the vaulted corridor known as the Cloisters, off which is the chapel with its late 17th-century rich plaster ceiling. In addition to the high fan-vaulted ceiling and marble inset fireplace in the adjoining schoolroom, look out for the embroidered stools, which were worked by Sir Roger's first wife, Sophia Conyers.

Past the Little Sitting Room is the Saloon, which has amazing plaster hanging loops and lace-like tracery in its ceiling. The room also has full-length portraits of Sir Roger and his second wife, Hester Mundy. There is another spectacular ceiling, this one barrel-vaulted, in the drawing room.

Outside, the informal gardens, extending away from the house, are a real joy.

Elegant plasterwork and statuary are features of the dining room at Arbury Hall

99

BODRHYDDAN HALL Denbighshire

3 miles (5km) south of Rhyl | Open selected afternoons June to September | Tel: 01745 590414 | www.bodrhyddan.co.uk

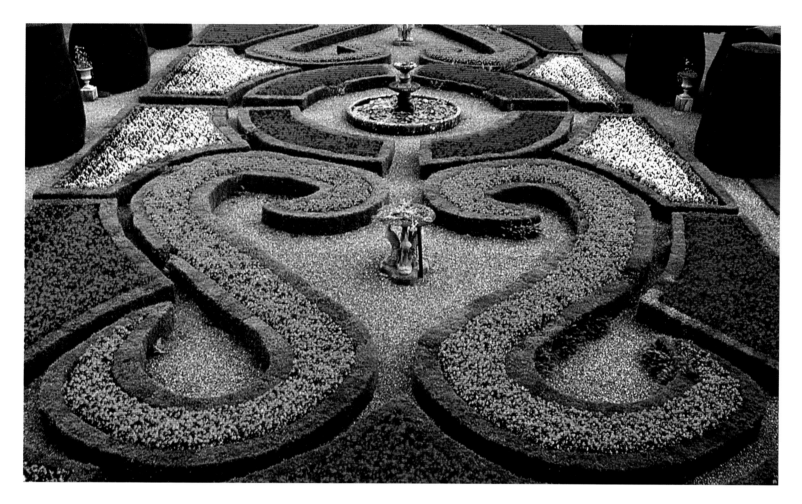

The formal gardens at Bodrhyddan Hall are a riot of colour and pattern

Only a few miles from the North Wales coast, near Abergele, is Bodrhyddan Hall, in its own lovely parkland. It is probable that there has been a house on the site for 700 years, and certainly Bodrhyddan has been in the hands of the same family, the Rowley-Conwys, for that long. The first dwelling was probably of wattle and daub, and substantial parts of its 15th-century successor are incorporated in the present house, including the inner walls of the Great Hall, the cellar doorway, and Tudor stone flags in the Gun Room.

It was with Sir Henry Conwy, during the Commonwealth and Restoration periods, that the status of the family was enhanced.

Though his loyalties have never been recorded, it would seem that he worked secretly for the King while engaged by Cromwell as High Sheriff of Flintshire. After the Restoration, Sir Henry was given a baronetcy by Charles II and it was this elevation that prompted his plans to rebuild the family home – plans that were actually carried out by his son John.

Over the garden entrance, a date stone shows that Sir John Conwy built the house between 1696 and 1700. This was a mellow brick structure, with stone quoins, that comprises most of the present south front; it was approached up the old drive, which is

now a grassy avenue. Sir John's two-storeyed house was built in typical William and Mary style, with the Great Hall as its central feature. Towards the end of the 18th century, the Big Dining Room was constructed, probably by Dean Shipley, who married the heiress of Bodrhyddan. In 1872, the house was enlarged for Conwy Grenville Hercules Rowley-Conwy by William Eden Nesfield, who added picturesque wings at each end, making the new main entrance face west, with a mile-long drive running down towards Rhuddlan.

BURGHLEY HOUSE Lincolnshire

Burghley, the greatest of England's Elizabethan houses, was built in fits and starts, mostly from 1574 onwards. Its builder was William Cecil, Elizabeth I's Lord Treasurer, her chief minister for forty years and, from 1571, her Lord Burghley. He wanted a palace, full of splendour and visual drama, grand enough to entertain monarchs – and he got his wish. Burghley House is Renaissance without really being classical, and signalled a robustly English route for the architectural fashion of the age – an exuberant, uninhibited Gothic romanticism, full of riotous decoration and without the rigid symmetry found in its Continental counterparts.

The scale of the building is such that it can carry this diversity. In appearance it is not so much a house as a small city, set in the little principality of its walled park. Each of the four main elevations is different, ringing wide changes on a basic structural grid. Its projecting corner towers, crowned by turrets with cupolas, contrive to unify it. Its roofline is broken by a riot of ornate stair-towers, chimney stacks in the shape of tall, paired Ionic columns, all manner of decorative finials and a pyramid-shaped obelisk that might at first sight be mistaken for the spire of a parish church. All this is indeed meant to impress, and impress from a distance – as it does when seen through Jean Tijou's superb wrought-iron, gilded west gates. These gates were, in fact, commissioned by a later Cecil, John, 5th Earl of Exeter, who, in the last quarter of the 17th century, combed Europe for pictures, tapestries and furniture to adorn his house. He also recruited the finest craftsmen from far and wide: the Frenchman, Tijou, the painter Louis Laguerre, that prince among wood-carvers, Grinling Gibbons, with his pupils, and yet another painter, the Italian Antonio Verrio, fresh from the royal palaces of Windsor and Hampton Court.

In the 18th century, the 9th Earl enlisted 'Capability' Brown to redesign the grounds and make changes to the buildings in a way that he felt would be respectful of the 5th Earl's improvements.

The imposing facade of Burghley House, with its spires and tall chimneys, is impressive from a distance

CALKE ABBEY Derbyshire

🐓 8 miles (13km) south of Derby | Open selected afternoons February to October | Tel: 01332 863822 | **www.nationaltrust.org.uk**

Calke Abbey is, perhaps, one of the few places that can rightly claim to be unique. It is certainly different from the usual stately home, and this is largely due to the family who occupied it for more than 300 years. A former Augustinian priory was an appropriate choice of home for the Harpurs, who were noted for their reclusive tendencies. With a sizeable fortune made from the law in Elizabethan time, the Harpurs lavished money on updating the Tudor house, first in baroque style, later in neoclassical style.

Sir Vauncey Harpur's bedroom (left) and the schoolroom (above) are mid-19th-century treasures

It was Sir Henry Harpur (1763–1819) who compounded the reclusive label that still attaches to his family name. He somewhat pretentiously adopted the name of the Crewe barons, distant relations by marriage, and renamed his home – but then spoilt the whole effect by marrying a lady's maid, and was ostracized by his contemporaries.

Sir Henry's great-grandson was another character: Sir Vauncey Harpur Crewe had an overriding passion for natural history, to the extent of hanging hunting trophies over his bed. His collection of stuffed creatures, birds' eggs, shells and walking sticks add to the eccentricities to be found around the house. The landscaped park includes a walled garden, and a vegetable garden on the site of the former physic garden.

Outbuildings at the side of the house include a brewhouse, linked to the house by a tunnel. In the stableyard old carriages and farm implements remain.

The National Trust, which acquired the property in 1985, have managed to carry out essential repairs to the house while retaining its 'time capsule' appearance.

CHARLECOTE PARK Warwickshire

A popular story has it that the young William Shakespeare was apprehended for poaching deer in the park at Charlecote and that this was the reason for his quick departure to the fleshpots of London.

An imposing two-storey Elizabethan gateway, complete with balustrading and corner towers topped by cupolas, is a more than suitable introduction to the beautiful 16th-century home of the Lucy family. They came to this country with William the Conqueror, and Charlecote has been the family home since the 12th century, although the present house was built around 1551. It still looks Elizabethan, but this is largely due to 19th-century nostalgia for days gone by. George Hammond Lucy, who inherited the house in 1823, swept away all the changes that the intervening generations had made and recreated the original style in consultation with an antiquarian specialist.

The Great Hall is particularly convincing, though its barrel-vaulted ceiling is plaster painted to look like timber, and the hall is now a superb showcase for family portraits. The largest, hung above the fireplace, is a delightful representation of Sir Thomas Lucy III and his family.

Elsewhere there are ornamented plaster ceilings above richly coloured wallpaper and wood panelling, magnificent pieces of furniture – the most startling must be the hugely ornate bed in the Ebony Bedroom, which was made from a 17th-century East Indian settee – and fine works of art. In contrast, the range of domestic buildings includes the kitchen, scullery, laundry, brewhouse and a coach house, still with a collection of family coaches.

Top right: The gatehouse is the only Elizabethan feature at Charlecote to survive completely unaltered

Right: Ceramics bought by George Hammond Lucy from the 1823 Fonthill sale

CHATSWORTH Derbyshire

3 miles (5km) east of Bakewell | Open daily except Christmas period | Tel: 01246 565300 | www.chatsworth.org

Visitors have come to Chatsworth since the first house was built here in 1552 by the redoubtable Bess of Hardwick and her second husband, Sir William Cavendish. Two husbands on, Bess had Mary, Queen of Scots in the house several times as a prisoner. Little was done to update what must have already been a magnificent Elizabethan house until her Cavendish successors – created Dukes of Devonshire in 1694 for helping William of Orange to the throne – added a new south front in 1687.

Once rebuilding started, the other four sides were rapidly converted in rich classical style between 1700 and 1705. A century later the 6th Duke added a huge new north wing, with rooms even grander than those of the earlier building, which became 'a museum of old furniture and a walk in wet weather.'

Impressive though Chatsworth is from the outside – the treasures inside are overwhelming. Painted gods swirl dizzily overhead in the monumental Painted Hall. The Great Stairs (one of seventeen staircases in the house) lead to the 1st Duke's state rooms on the second floor. The 6th Duke thought them all 'useless display' and wanted to make bedrooms out of the whole lot, but

these were never rooms for relaxed living. Instead, they display the awesome wealth and power of the Cavendishes, with superb carved panelling, lavishly painted ceilings and priceless objects at every turn. The overall impression is of polished wood, gold leaf and rich fabrics. Don't miss the trompe l'oeil violin apparently hanging on a door in the Music Room. The chapel looks just as it did three centuries ago, and you can almost see the curly wigged courtiers of Charles on the stiff-backed chairs; the library, once the Long Gallery, took shape in the 1830s, and prepares us for the enormous dining room –

Left: The west front at Chatsworth

Above: The West Sketch Gallery

Right: Bust of Palladio in the West Sketch Gallery

like an outpost of Buckingham Palace – and the 6th Duke's Sculpture Gallery, a rather chilly assembly of neoclassical marbles.

Chatsworth's gardens, too, merit superlatives. There is formality, with the rectangular Canal Pond and its huge Emperor Fountain. The Cascade has tumbled down the hillside since 1696, when the copper Willow Tree fountain, designed to spray unwary visitors, was already in place. More informal are the rockeries, including the waterfall that tumbles 45 feet (14m) over the Wellington Rock, the grotto and the tree-lined slopes of the arboretum, all conjured up by Paxton's magic.

DEENE PARK Northamptonshire

Standing in carefully tended gardens in rural Northamptonshire, Deene Park was acquired by Sir Robert Brudenell in 1514, and has been the family home ever since. The house boasts many fine features. The Great Hall has original 16th-century panelling and an impressive hammer-beam roof. The 17th-century stained glass was badly damaged when an American warplane, complete with bombs, crashed nearby; it wasn't repaired until 1959.

The first Brudenell to own Deene Park, Sir Robert, was a lawyer who invested his large fortune in land. His grandson Edmund married an heiress, but they were unhappy.

She died after a long illness, and Edmund's ghost is said to haunt the house, full of remorse for his neglect and infidelity.

The Bow Room now houses a magnificent collection of 16th- and 17th-century books. Many of them belonged to the 1st Earl of Cardigan, who lost them temporarily when Deene Park was sacked by Cromwell's troops during the Civil War. To his fury, the Earl was made to buy them back when the war was over. The White Hall contains a painting by James Sant of the 7th Earl describing the Charge of the Light Brigade to Prince Albert and his children. The story goes that Queen

Deene Park is surrounded by glorious gardens, much improved during the last thirty years

Victoria was originally included in the picture, but insisted on being removed after being scandalized by the Earl's flagrant affair with his mistress. The 7th Earl's widow died in 1915 and towards the end of her life the house began to fall into disrepair, mainly due to the expense of its upkeep. It was used to billet soldiers during World War II, and by 1946 had degenerated into a sad condition. However, since then it has been painstakingly restored to its former glory.

DODDINGTON HALL Lincolnshire

Doddington Hall is a particularly fine Elizabethan E-shaped house in local stone and pink brick, dug and fired on site, with chimneys and domed gazebos rising above its roof parapet. It was built in 1600 for Thomas Taylor, the Bishop of Lincoln's registrar, by Robert Smythson, architect of Hardwick Hall, Wollaton and other great Midlands houses. Externally, the house remains much as it was built – thanks largely to the sensitive care of its Georgian owner, John Delaval.

Most of the rooms – notably the Great Hall, drawing room, Imperial Staircase and Long Gallery – are early Georgian in style, while the library and parlour retain Queen Anne panelling and decorations. These rooms are filled with beautiful furniture, pictures, porcelain and textiles, in marked contrast with the original sparse interiors revealed by an inventory taken when the first Thomas Taylor died in 1606. There were then only eighty-five pieces of furniture spread over a total of forty rooms!

The house passed from the Taylors by marriage, first to the Hussey family and then to the Delavels of Seaton Delaval, who owned the house until 1830. At this time the Jarvis family inherited the estate as a result of a romantic attachment in Dover between George Ralph Payne Jarvis and Sarah, the widowed Delavel heiress.

The house is approached through a Dutch-gabled Tudor gatehouse and across the East Garden Courtyard. The gardens nearest the house are walled, formal and traditional; beyond are more natural areas, with a very convincing Temple of the Winds – built with his own hands by the present Mr Antony Jarvis to mark his father's sixty-fifth birthday.

Doddington Hall's mellow brick exterior with its walled courtyards has barely changed over the centuries

107

EASTNOR CASTLE Herefordshire

2½ miles (4km) south east of Ledbury | Open selected days April to September | Tel: 01531 633160 | www.eastnorcastle.com

At the time when lawyer John Cocks, the 2nd Baron Somers, was seeking a rapid passage into the aristocracy, the size and splendour of the family home were seen as key indicators of status and fortune. His strategic investment in a castle had the desired effect, for soon after its completion he became the 1st Earl of Somers.

Eastnor Castle was completed in 1824 for £85,923. 13s. 1d. The symmetrical design was by Robert Smirke, later the architect of the British Museum, who chose to create a Norman Revival style fortress at Eastnor, with simple Gothic interiors. Gothic enthusiast Augustus Pugin was commissioned to decorate the drawing room in the High Gothic style in the 1850s – the furniture, the lavish chimneypiece, and the great iron chandelier are all his work. More embellishment was commissioned by Charles, the 3rd Earl Somers, over the next two decades.

Many of the items on display at Eastnor were collected during the long travels of the 3rd Earl. Something of a connoisseur, he collected Italian furniture, Flemish tapestries, Renaissance art, arms and armour. He also acquired a stunningly beautiful half-French wife, Virginia Pattle, reputedly falling in love with her when he saw her portrait by Watts, which is now in the Little Library. She and her seven sisters were known as 'Pattledom', and this vivacious group were welcomed with open arms by London's artistic elite. One of the sisters was the photographer Julia Margaret Cameron, and some of her work is also on display in the house. The excitement and glamour of partying with the likes of Tennyson, Browning and Ellen Terry was a far cry from Eastnor, and Virginia rarely visited the castle, though her two daughters were brought up there.

Over-the-top Gothic splendour in the drawing room of Eastnor Castle

ELTON HALL Cambridgeshire

An avenue of lime trees leads to the front of this splendid palace, which looks more like a French chateau than an English country house. The back of Elton Hall is even more glorious – a Gothic extravaganza of turrets, battlements, pinnacles and pointed windows.

There has been a house where Elton Hall now stands since the Norman Conquest. The earliest parts of the present house are the 15th-century gatehouse and a chapel with fine fan vaulting. These were later incorporated in Sir Thomas Proby's Jacobean building, completed in 1666. A hundred years later, more buildings were added using labour from French prisoners of war, but most of this work was undone by the architect Henry Ashton in the mid-1800s. Seventy years later, the 4th Earl of Carysfort added the large central tower and some more rooms, so that the remaining house is a mixture of styles.

The guided tours lead visitors through room after room of treasures gathered over 300 years. Paintings by Gainsborough, Hobbema, Poussin, Henry O'Neill and Constable vie for attention with Louis XV cabinets and 18th-century ceilings. Also outstanding among the contents of the Hall is the library, which contains some early bibles

Elton Hall's rose garden dates from the 15th century, when the house was built for Sir Richard Sapcote

and psalters, including a prayer book owned and inscribed by Henry VIII and two of his wives. In stark contrast to the cosy book-lined walls of the library is the flamboyant white and gold drawing room, designed by Ashton. Gilded chairs are covered by Beauvais tapestry, while the walls are hung with paintings by Reynolds, Allan Ramsay and Hoppner. The adjacent Octagon Room, in Strawberry Hill 'Gothick' style, contains cases of delicate Sèvres porcelain.

109

ERDDIG Wrexham

No-one, least of all the National Trust, who now have the care of Erddig, would claim that this house is an architectural masterpiece, but its importance today and its source of fascination to visitors lies in the vivid insight it provides into the social and working life of a great country house.

In recognition of this, the tour of the house and estate begins at the working end of the scale, where the carpenters, blacksmiths, stablehands and laundry maids toiled away through their working lives. The workshops are fully equipped and the sawmill building has a display of photographs and a video showing the extent of the restoration work carried out at Erddig.

After passing through the kitchens and servants' hall, visitors reach the grand neoclassical rooms that were occupied by the Yorke family until the 1970s. They are still furnished with the wonderful collection of gilt and silver furniture amassed by John Mellor, ancestor of the Yorkes, who bought Erddig from its original owner in 1716. Perhaps the most remarkable piece of furniture is the shining gold and cream state bed, with Chinese silk hangings. It was very nearly lost when the house was in a bad state of

View across the Victorian Parterre (above) and the New Kitchen, built in the early 1770s (right)

repair, and rain poured through the collapsing plaster ceiling of the bedroom through the canopy and into buckets placed on the bed! However, after two years in the conservation department of the Victoria and Albert Museum this magnificent piece of furniture has been restored to its original condition.

In contrast are the sparsely furnished attic bedrooms where the maids slept, and the nearby workroom where they spent their rare moments of leisure.

EUSTON HALL Norfolk

3 miles (5km) south east of Thetford | Open selected days mid-June to mid-September | Tel: 01842 766366 | **www.eustonhall.co.uk**

In 1902 a great fire raged at Euston Hall. The south and west wings were gutted, destroying, among other priceless treasures, the 18th-century ceilings painted by Verrio. Only the north wing remained. The burned wings were quickly rebuilt, but were demolished in 1952 so that the Hall that can be seen today dates mainly from the 1740s.

The house was originally built between 1666 and 1670 for the Duke of Arlington, Charles II's Secretary of State and a loyal supporter of the Stuart cause. He made a splendid match for his daughter Isabella when she was only five years old, betrothing her to Henry FitzRoy, the illegitimate son of the King and his mistress Barbara Villiers. Henry FitzRoy was made the Duke of Grafton,

and Euston Hall, which he inherited from Arlington, has been the family home of the Graftons ever since.

Euston Hall was probably one of the first English country houses to have the luxury of a mechanically pumped water supply. The diarist John Evelyn visited Euston in 1671, and commented on the 'pretty engine' that pumped an abundant supply of water from a nearby canal for all the house's needs, with enough left over to run the fountains and a corn mill.

Henry FitzRoy enjoyed his inheritance for only five years before he died. His son, the 2nd Duke, then commissioned Matthew Brettingham to remodel the house. Brettingham decided to face all three wings

with red brick, as well as building the stable block in 1750–55, and these buildings remained untouched until the disaster of the fire in 1902.

Euston Hall possesses a magnificent collection of 17th-century courtly paintings. Since Henry FitzRoy's origins were indisputably Stuart, Stuart portraits fill every corner of the house. Charles I's painting is by Van Dyck, and those of Charles II and Barbara Villiers are by Lely. The portrait of Nell Gwyn, who was Barbara's famous rival for Charles II's affections, hangs rather unceremoniously in a side corridor.

A victim of fire damage, most of what we see today at Euston Hall dates from the 1740s

EYAM HALL Derbyshire

Plague put the village of Eyam on the map in 1665. Part of Eyam Hall was already in existence, but this typical Derbyshire manor dates mostly from 1671, when Thomas Wright, a forebear of the present owners, built it for his son John.

The building has changed little since the Wrights' day. It is modest in size, part of the village rather than standing aloof, and gives the impression that the family must always have been in the thick of local affairs. Behind its elegant gateway on the village street its entrance front, with two solid wings and central doorway, has leaded windows that add glittering life to a restrained facade. Once inside, the comfortable prosperity of the building is all-embracing. The large entrance

hall sets the tone, with its beamed ceiling and wide 18th-century fireplace. Two huge settles on either side of the fire have been in the house since at least 1694, and in the rare 17th-century cedar coffer the present owners discovered early bed hangings – some can be seen elsewhere in the house. Major John Wright, whose swaggering portrait hangs here, served in America in 1777. The staircase, probably Jacobean, may have come from another house; but romantic tradition says that the heart it incorporates was for John Wright and his bride Elizabeth when they moved into their new home.

The Tapestry Room is hung with examples of several different periods, including a 15th-century Flemish tapestry. Several have been

Eyam Hall and its charming grounds are an integral part of the village of Eyam

unceremoniously cut up to fill the walls, like draught-proof wallpaper. Engraved on the library window is an 18th-century poem in praise of Fanny Holme, 'ye pride of natures beauteous Powers', but as she never married into the family, she presumably never occupied the magnificent 17th-century bed, with its solid wooden roof, in the next room. In the dining room, once part of the original kitchen, the table is set for a Victorian dinner party, while in the kitchen proper the present owners have uncovered the fireplace of around 1700 and furnished the room with old kitchen implements.

113

GRIMSTHORPE CASTLE Lincolnshire

3 miles (5km) north west of Bourne | Open selected days April to September | Tel: 01778 591205 | **www.grimsthorpe.co.uk**

Grimsthorpe, with its great avenue, the Chestnut Riding, lake and fishpond, deer park and woodlands, is one of eastern England's most imposing houses. Though called 'castle', it is really an 18th-century palace, designed for the Duke of Ancaster by that most dramatic of architects, Sir John Vanbrugh. It was the last great house he designed.

The estate has its origins in a Norman castle and nearby Cistercian abbey, both built of stone quarried here. Little remains of the monastery; its stone was reused for the castle, which was substantially rebuilt in the 14th, 17th and 18th centuries. Its oldest part is the 12th-century King John's Tower at its south-east corner which, though considerably restored, still has arrow slits and some walls 7 feet (2m) thick.

It was around 1533 that Charles Brandon, forty-nine-year-old Duke of Suffolk, married his fourteen-year-old ward Katherine, Baroness Willoughby de Eresby. Brandon used stone from the abbey to convert the medieval castle into a commodious Tudor courtyard house. His 17th-century descendant, the 14th Lord, who fought for Charles II in the Civil War, partly rebuilt it during the Restoration, but the big rebuilding came after George I had created the 16th Lord the 1st Duke of Ancaster.

The new duke commissioned Sir John Vanbrugh, architect of Blenheim and Castle Howard, to transform the castle into a palace, but did not live to see it completed. His son presided over the building of Vanbrugh's new north front before funds dried up. Yet what was achieved transformed Grimsthorpe. The palatial north front is typical of Vanbrugh, a dramatist as well as an architect. Its skyline is topped by balustraded towers, ornate chimneys and statues; the grand courtyard in front is enclosed by wing walls lined with niches and ending in corner pavilions that echo the main towers. Completing the ensemble is a splendid iron grille and gates.

Imposing Grimsthorpe Castle, seen above the rose parterre, was one of Sir John Vanbrugh's finest works

HADDON HALL

1½ miles (2.5km) south of Bakewell | Open selected afternoons April to December | Tel: 01629 812855 | **www.haddonhall.co.uk**

'All Derbyshire is but a world of peaked hills which from some of the highest you discover the rest like steeples ... as thick as can be,' wrote that indefatigable traveller Celia Fiennes when she visited the county in 1697. Yet this inhospitable landscape has long cradled two of the most remarkable houses in England – the princely Chatsworth and, just over the hill, Haddon. For 200 years Haddon slumbered like the Sleeping Beauty's castle. It was kept ticking over, repaired where necessary, but as changes of taste swirled around it – as the fashions for baroque, Palladian, neoclassical or High Victorian laid their sometimes heavy hand on other houses – Haddon remained unchanged, its grey towers with their blanket of ivy floating magically over the dense trees, as if waiting for their Prince Charming to appear and breathe the breath of life into them once again.

Like all the best fairy stories, Haddon's tale has a happy ending, for Prince Charming did come, though he was a Duke rather than a prince. The 9th Duke of Rutland, while still the Marquis of Granby, came back to Haddon at the beginning of the 20th century and began its restoration. The care with which it had been kept since the 1700s meant that his task, which he carried out with enormous sympathy, not just for the structure of the house but also for its unique atmosphere, was less daunting than it might have been. The Duke (he succeeded his father in 1925) insisted on two things – that as much as possible should be preserved in the house, and that, where it was necessary to replace, the highest standards of craftsmanship were to be used. Work began in 1920, and by his death in 1940 he had seen beauty awaken at Haddon once again.

The fairytale exterior (top) and the interior of Haddon Hall (right) have a haunting beauty

HAGLEY HALL West Midlands

The serene exterior of Hagley Hall. Today the house is a very popular wedding venue

Hagley Hall has been in the Lyttelton family for nine generations, and the family has held this land since 1564. This last of the great Palladian houses is largely the creation of George, 1st Lord Lyttelton. Secretary to and chief favourite of Frederick, Prince of Wales, he was a poet, man of letters, politician and briefly Chancellor of the Exchequer (1755–56). George acquired his Italianate taste on his Grand Tour of 1728–31, and this is reflected in the house, which he had built between 1756 and 1760. He celebrated its completion with a three-day house-warming party, and the house remains much as it was

then. Although there has been a park here since the 14th century, the present landscape with its follies and rotunda was created in the eleven years up to 1758. Amiable, absent-minded, but a model of integrity, George Lyttelton's character is a marked contrast to that of his son, Thomas. Commonly called 'the wicked Lord Lyttelton' ('Naughty Tom' to the family) he was remarkably badly behaved, and was a founder member of Sir Francis Dashwood's notorious Hell Fire Club. After marrying Apphia Peach, widow of a former Governor of Calcutta, he published some pious verses in her honour, then ran

off to Paris with a barmaid, though he did return to sit in the House of Lords.

Hagley Hall's splendid interiors include the intricate plasterwork of the White Hall, the spectacular rococo ceiling by Vassalli in the dining room and, best of all, the marvellously preserved Soho arabesque tapestries of the drawing room. In the 19th century the columned Gallery was found to be ideal for family cricket practice, with inevitably damaging results!

HARDWICK HALL Derbyshire

4½ miles (7km) north west of Mansfield | Open selected afternoons spring to autumn | Tel: 01246 850430 | www.nationaltrust.org.uk

Elizabeth, Countess of Shrewsbury – 'Bess of Hardwick' – was a remarkable and very shrewd woman. She came from a fairly modest background and proceeded to outlive her four husbands, each richer and higher up the social scale than the one before. With her wealth, Bess built great houses, including Chatsworth, but Hardwick Hall – built on a hilltop between Chesterfield and Mansfield – was the last, begun when she was seventy, after the death of her fourth husband, the Earl of Shrewsbury, in 1590.

With architect Robert Smythson (whose work can also be seen at Longleat and Wollaton Hall), Bess created an impressive mansion with enormous windows and six great towers surmounted by her ornately fashioned monogram – 'ES'. One of the first English houses to have the Great Hall built on an axis through the centre of the house, instead of at right angles to the entrance,

it consists of three main stories, each one higher than the one below. A grand stone staircase leads to the state rooms on the second floor. The Hall was designed specifically to house the collection of tapestries that still line its walls, and the Long Gallery, running the length of the east front, is hung with family portraits.

When Bess died in 1608 Hardwick passed to her grandson William Cavendish, who bought his brother's share in Chatsworth and made this the principal family seat. Thus Hardwick Hall was left quite unaltered by succeeding generations.

As well as being a splendid example of its age, Hardwick has some particularly important works of embroidery, some worked by Bess herself, others by Mary, Queen of Scots, who was confined here for a time. The sumptuous embroidery of the bedhead in the state bedroom is an outstanding example.

Sunlight warms the roof of the Elizabethan Hall built in 1591–97 (above). Elizabeth I (below) was a frequent visitor. She was painted here by Nicholas Hilliard

HEDINGHAM CASTLE Essex

4 miles (6km) north of Halstead | Open selected days April to October | Tel: 01787 460261 | **www.hedinghamcastle.co.uk**

The vast tower of Hedingham Castle looms over the surrounding countryside as a great monument to the Norman Conquest. The original Saxon owner of the title of lordship of Hedingham was dispossessed by William, and given to Aubrey de Vere. Aubrey's son, Aubrey II, built the huge tower around 1140, using the Archbishop of Canterbury as his architect. It is 73 feet (22m) high, with a further 20 feet (6m) gained by the two corner turrets. There are four floors, although the enormous Great Hall is twice as high as the other storeys. The entire building is faced with Ashlar stone, which, since it was very expensive to transport, is an indication of the great wealth of the early de Veres.

Norman towers were designed for strength and defence, and Hedingham is no exception. The main entrance is on the first floor, not the ground floor, so that attackers would find it more difficult to enter. The walls of the keep are between 10 and 12 feet (3–3.5m) thick, to provide protection against battering rams, undermining and missiles. Small rooms and passages are built into the thickness of the walls, many with arrow slits through which invaders could be attacked.

The massive chamber on the second floor houses the largest Norman arch in Europe. This magnificent arch is 28 feet (8.5m) across and 20 feet (6m) high. The chamber's arched windows and doorways are richly carved, and there is a gallery running around the entire room in the thickness of the walls. There is no evidence that there was either a chapel or a kitchen in the tower. The absence of the latter is understandable, for one of the biggest hazards to castle dwellers was fire, and it is likely that the cooking and baking buildings were outside the main tower for safety reasons.

Built for defence rather than gracious living, Hedingham Castle dates from the Norman Conquest

119

HELLENS Herefordshire

Hellens is a rather dilapidated house with a thrilling history, and there are reminders of its story throughout the house. For example, James Audley, grandson of Yseult Mortimer Audley, was a life-long friend of Edward III's son, the Black Prince, and a monumental fireplace (still visible) in the lobby was decorated with the Prince's crest in honour of his visit. The Prince and his youngbloods are said to have held a raucous banquet here just before they sailed for the Battle of Poitiers in 1356. James rented the house from his uncle for a yearly payment of 'a pair of gilt spurs to be given at Easter'. One of these pairs can be seen at the top of the stairway.

For centuries, the inheritance of Hellens followed a wandering course, mainly down the female line. Then it came to Hilda Pennington-Mellor, who married Swedish doctor and philanthropist, Axel Munthe, and bore him two sons; their descendants live in the house today. Displayed among the many portraits in the lobby is a Flemish tapestry used as a tarpaulin to cover the Protestant family's goods when they fled Catholic Belgium in the 16th century.

The Staircase Hall was last decorated in the 17th century as part of a major modernization for the marriage in 1641 of the guardian's fifteen-year-old daughter, Margaret, to sixteen-year-old Fulke Walwyn. During the Civil War, Fulke gathered all the bravest men in Much Marcle and led them away, through the big gates and through Hellens' parkland to Ledbury, where a terrible battle took place. Margaret watched him go with great foreboding in her heart, and vowed that no-one should ever pass through that gate until her beloved Fulke returned. Sadly, they remain locked to this day. The house was subsequently taken over by Roundheads, who chased Fulke's Catholic chaplain around the house, cornering and killing him in the Queen's Room. His ghost is said to haunt Hellens. The estate was later returned to the family.

Fulke's cousin, Lady Mary Wharton, later owned Hellens, and at the top of the staircase is a snuff box which once belonged to her nephew Philip, Duke of Wharton. He died in disgrace after a life devoted to carousing, black magic and intrigue. Mehetabble Walwyn's Room is named after a woman who fled Hellens with a lover, and later returned humiliated to live out her days behind the barred windows of the room.

The East Front (left) and the Court Room (right) seen from the Minstrel's Gallery

HOLKHAM HALL Norfolk

Holkham Hall sprawls majestically in its 3,000-acre (1,1214-ha) park a mile from the wild and windswept north Norfolk coast. At the turn of the 17th century, the land on which the Hall now stands was little more than a desolate heathland. When Thomas Coke told his friends where he planned to build his home, many reacted with horror. That the designs for Coke's new house were inspired by buildings he had admired in the warm and gentle climate of Italy made his choice of location even stranger.

Today, as the visitor strolls across the rich lawns and enjoys the shade of abundant oaks and beeches, it is difficult to imagine that it was once an uncultivated heath. Some of the trees were planted as early as 1712 in anticipation of the splendid park that was to follow. Visitors may picnic next to the peaceful lake or wander through acres of landscaped gardens and parklands. Or they may prefer to admire architect William Kent's great obelisk or the monument to the architectural achievements of 'Coke of Norfolk'. But at the centre of all this is the resplendent Hall itself, offering the visitor the chance to see 2,000 years of fine art, all housed in one of the largest and most grand 18th-century palaces in the world. Holkham is one of the finest examples of Palladian revival architecture in England, with room after room of glittering splendour. Everywhere, there is evidence of Kent's outstanding talent, especially in the exquisitely carved scrolls, shells, cherubs and flowers on the ceilings, the walls and the furnishings. Coke's state rooms show off his incredible collection of art, and dazzle the visitor with Palladian magnificence.

Holkham Hall's wonderfully grand staircase is just a taste of its dazzling architecture

HOUGHTON HALL Norfolk

Sir Robert Walpole, 1st Earl of Orford, and Prime Minister of England from 1730 to 1741, was born in 1676. While he was First Lord of the Treasury and Chancellor, his brother-in-law and ally, Charles, 2nd Viscount Townshend, was Secretary of State, and between them they wielded a formidable amount of power. When the relationship between these powerful men began to break down, Walpole's decision to build himself a glittering new palace at Houghton, a mere 10 miles (16km) from Townshend's ancestral seat of Raynham Hall, infuriated Townshend.

By the time Walpole became Prime Minister, he had managed to engineer Townshend's resignation from the government, and Townshend retired to Raynham in bitter defeat. While Walpole lavishly entertained his influential friends from government and politics at Houghton, Townshend left the area altogether, and refused all invitations to visit.

But Walpole did not spend all his time at Houghton eating, drinking and hunting. He built up a fine collection of paintings of Old Masters, as well as vast collections of furniture and sculpture. After his death in 1745, his feckless grandson sold most of the pictures to Catherine the Great, and they now grace the walls of the Hermitage Museum in St Petersburg. In 1797, Houghton passed to the Cholmondeley family, but it was not until 1913 that this magnificent palace became their permanent home.

Building at Houghton Hall was started in 1721 on the site of two earlier houses. The village of Houghton was demolished, and its inhabitants relocated outside the park gates; it then became known as New Houghton. It was not unusual in the 18th century for villages to be moved to suit their landlords. Walpole's house was originally designed by Colen Campbell, but James Gibbs added the cupola-like domes at each corner, and

The marble hallway inside Houghton Hall is known as William Kent's masterpiece of design

suggested that the main building material should be hard-wearing yellow sandstone brought by sea from Whitby.

Walpole left the entire interior design to William Kent, who added marble fireplaces, carved woodwork, many of the murals and much of the furniture. Kent's masterpiece is the cube-shaped 'stone hall', which has a plaster ceiling frieze by Atari and Bugutti,

and reliefs over the fireplace and door by Michael Rysbrack. The other state rooms are also splendid. One of the dressing rooms is hung with rare Mortlake tapestries, while the Regency White Drawing Room has Louis XV tables laden with Sèvres porcelain.

INGATESTONE HALL Essex

Portraits, wooden ceiling beams and wood panelling inside Ingatestone Hall

In 1535, Thomas Cromwell's assistant, a young lawyer called William Petre, prowled southern England persuading monasteries and abbeys to give up their riches to the King. When he reached Barking Abbey, he took a liking to its manor of Yenge-atte-Stone (Ingatestone). After the Dissolution of the Monasteries, Petre bought the manor for £849. 12s. 6d. Simultaneously he endowed an almshouse for the poor so that, in the eyes of the Pope, his purchase would not be construed as plundering church property.

Petre built himself a fine house befitting his rising position at Court. His son, John, bought nearby Thorndon Hall, and the two houses remained in the Petre family for the next 300 years. William was appointed Secretary of State by Henry VIII, and he remained in this office until ill-health forced him to retire in the reign of Elizabeth I. He has been described as the 'first civil servant', and also refounded Exeter College, Oxford. William's son, John, was made 1st Lord Petre by James I, and was one of the patrons of the composer William Byrd. His great-grandson, the 4th Lord, was implicated in the 'Popish Plot' of Titus Oates and died in the Tower of London. The Petre family retained their Catholic beliefs, even through the Commonwealth years. The 9th Lord was a prominent figure in the movement for Catholic emancipation in the 18th century, and his great-great-grandson, the 13th Lord, was ordained priest.

In the 18th century, Ingatestone's old west wing was demolished, the whole house was 'modernized' with corridors and sash windows, and the house was divided into self-contained apartments that were rented out. The 16th Lord Petre died in the Great War, and in 1919 his wife began the restoration of Ingatestone.

KEDLESTON HALL Derbyshire

5 miles (8km) north west of Derby | Open selected afternoons February to November | Tel: 01332 842191 | www.nationaltrust.org.uk

Many grand mansions claim to be the finest example of the work of the brilliant Scottish architect, Robert Adam, but Kedleston Hall is well up in the running. Its planning, however, began as something of a muddle.

Sir Nathanial Curzon, who inherited the estate in 1758, accepted a design submitted by Matthew Brettingham and James Paine; they had already built the pavilions and started on the ground floor of the main house when, in December 1758, Curzon was introduced to Robert Adam. He was so impressed by Adam's ideas that he gave him the job of directing and overseeing the work at Kedleston Hall.

The entrance front has been described as the grandest Palladian facade in Britain; at its centre is a vast Corinthian portico set on a high base with flights of steps on either side.

The interiors are no less impressive, and the first introduction is the magnificent Marble Hall, modelled on the ancient atrium of the classic Roman villa. The drawing room has a nautical theme, from the decorative plaster ceiling of grotesque sea creatures to the gilt settees carved with mermaids, tritons and dolphins. All around the house are fine works of art, including Old Masters, family portraits and superb furniture.

The Indian Museum has a fine display of furniture and artefacts collected by Lord Curzon when he served as Viceroy of India (1859–1925). Also on display is the dress – known as 'the peacock dress' for the hundreds of precious and semi-precious stones sewn into the fabric – worn by Lady Curzon at the 1903 Delhi Durbur Coronation.

The Marble Hall (left), designed by Robert Adam in the 1760s, was inspired by Roman architecture, while the Indian throne (below) was acquired by Lord Curzon

KENTWELL HALL Suffolk

4 miles (6km) north of Sudbury | Open selected afternoons April to September | Tel: 01787 310207 | www.kentwell.co.uk

In the Domesday Book, the manor of Kentwell was valued at £4 and was owned by Frodo, brother to the first Abbot of Bury St Edmund's. Nine hundred years later, the estate at Kentwell still survives, with the delightful Tudor manor house as its centrepiece. Built in soft red brick the Hall, which seems to change colour when viewed at different times of the day, is reached by an elegant avenue of lime trees that stretches almost a mile from the front gates, and surrounded by a wide moat.

The manor of Kentwell has been sold several times during its long history. It remained in Frodo's family until it passed to a family that took the name of the manor itself – the de Kentwells. By 1250, it was in the hands of King Henry III, who granted it to his half-brother, Sir William de Valence.

The Hall was owned briefly by the 14th-century poet John Gower, and eventually came to Sir William Clopton through his mother Katharine Mylde in 1403. William's son, John (1423–97), seems to have been responsible for the earliest parts of the existing complex.

Since 1972, the Hall and its gardens have undergone extensive restoration. Rooms on all three floors can be explored: the ground floor includes the Great Kitchen, the Panelled Room, Hopper's masterpieces, the 'Jacobethan' Main Dining Room, the Gothick Great Hall, the drawing room, the billiards room, the hall and the library. The various passages and staircases are also worthy of attention. On the top floor you will find the Victorian Room and the reformed State Bedroom, its boudoir converted into a Roman-style bathroom.

No visit to Kentwell would be complete without admiring the grounds. The rare-breeds farm is well worth a visit.

Kentwell Hall is a moated mellow red-brick mansion where many fascinating re-enactments take place

LAYER MARNEY TOWER Essex

On 22 April 1884, an earthquake shook eastern England. Chimneys toppled from Layer Marney Tower, and its walls and roofs were damaged, making it unsafe and virtually uninhabitable. Fortunately for Layer Marney, and for the thousands of visitors that admire it every year, the house has had a succession of caring owners who have gone to considerable effort and expense to ensure that it has been restored to its full glory.

The Marney family was first recorded here in 1166 and they remained until 1525. Henry Marney began building the tower in 1520, but died three years later, and his Renaissance courtyard mansion was never completed. The east and west wings adjoin the central tower, but the south side remains isolated from the rest of the house.

The tower is the tallest Tudor gatehouse in the country, and has two hexagonal turrets eight floors high with finely moulded brick topped with terracotta dolphins and shells. The use of terracotta, relatively recent in England, indicates Henry Marney's sophistication. Between the turrets are two spacious rooms with huge windows that may have been used as a royal suite.

Henry Marney served on the Privy Council during the reigns of Henry VII and VIII, where his sound advice and integrity earned him his knighthood in 1510, and his baronetcy in 1523. Sadly, he enjoyed his title for only six weeks before he died. His son John died two years later, and having no male heirs, the estate passed to the Tuke family. In 1580 it was sold to Sir Samuel Tyron, 1st Baronet of Layer Marney, after which a succession of owners included Nicholas Corsellis, whose memorial in Layer Marney church claims (falsely) that he had printed books five years before Caxton.

England's tallest Tudor gatehouse affords visitors magnificent views over the Blackwater estuary

LITTLE MALVERN COURT
Worcestershire

5 miles (8km) south of Great Malvern | Open selected afternoons April to July | Tel: 01684 892988 | **www.hha.org.uk**

Little Malvern Court is a manor house that includes the remains of its original medieval priory. After Henry VIII's Dissolution of the Monasteries, this priory was leased to John Russell, whose son Henry was granted the freehold in 1554 by Mary Tudor. The Russells maintained their Catholicism through centuries of opposition, worshipping in a secret chapel in the roof (now exposed). Early in the 18th century, ownership of Little Malvern was transferred by marriage to a member of another local Recusant family, Thomas Berington. His daughter Elizabeth was well known for the careful eye she kept on her finances – to the extent of charging her guests for food and lodging. Even her future husband, Thomas Williams, had to pay up during his first visit in April 1748. After the official opposition to Catholicism was relaxed in 1791, their daughter, Mary, converted the medieval Prior's Hall into a chapel.

In 1860 Joseph Hansom, designer of the famous cab, associate of Augustus Pugin and popular architect in Catholic circles, extended the house. This involved a new west wing, with dining room, drawing room and the west entrance hall. The funding came from Ellen Balfe, an heiress from County Roscommon in Ireland, who had met the owner, Charles Michael Berington, in Rome. She and her eight children all died within six years. The mournful Charles then considered becoming a monk, before marrying Patricia Mary Coxon, said to be an illicit descendant of Bonnie Prince Charlie.

The current owners, Tim and Alexandra Berington, have re-landscaped the garden, which is still dominated by a giant lime tree under which Queen Victoria played in 1831.

Little Malvern Court is surrounded by former monastic grounds, where Queen Victoria played as a child

MARGAM COUNTRY PARK

Close to the sea, between Porthcawl and Port Talbot, is Margam Country Park. The heart of this estate is the shell of the 19th-century mansion house, but the history of the area lies with the Abbey of Margam, founded in 1147 by Robert Consul, Earl of Gloucester. Given to the Cistercian monks from Clairvaux, the Abbey depended for its existence on sheep-rearing on the outlying granges worked by the lay brethren, much of the wool being exported to the Continent from nearby Taibach. Margam was one of the wealthiest abbeys in Wales during the 12th century, but, following the Black Death the numbers of lay brothers dwindled, and by 1536, when Henry VIII dissolved the monastery, only nine monks were left.

In 1536 Margam Abbey was bought by Sir Rice Mansel. Although a house was built incorporating part of the Abbey, this was demolished in the 18th century to make way for the famous orangery. His son, Christopher Rice Mansel Talbot, Liberal Member of Parliament for Glamorgan for sixty years from 1830, commissioned a large house from Thomas Hopper in 1830–35. It was one of Hopper's masterpieces, in the Tudor style, and built in warm red stone with a great octagonal tower, surmounted with pinnacles, rising in the middle. By 1941, however, the contents had been auctioned, and the mansion became derelict. Sadly it is now an empty shell and only the staircase is open to the public.

The orangery at Margam Park is one of the largest and most famous in the country. Built by Anthony Keck for Thomas Mansel Talbot between 1786 and 1790, it was intended to house the collection of orange, lemon and citrus trees inherited by the Talbots from their Mansel forebears.

The 19th-century house at the heart of Margam Country Park is surrounded by interesting grounds

MELBOURNE HALL Derbyshire

On the edge of Melbourne, 8 miles (13km) south of Derby | Open selected afternoons in August | Tel: 01332 862502 | **www.melbournehall.com**

In the 13th and 14th centuries, the Bishops of Carlisle came to Melbourne to escape the troublesome Scots, and used the superb Norman church next door to the Hall as their cathedral. From the 15th century the house was let to a succession of absentee landlords, including Thomas Cromwell, Lord Chancellor of England. Then, at the end of the 16th century, the current lessee, Sir Francis Needham, decided to make Melbourne Hall his home and set about making it habitable. A large part of the house was demolished and rebuilt, and the oldest part of the building we see today dates from that period.

The Hall was again altered considerably by Sir John Coke, Secretary of State to Charles I and ancestor of the hall's present owners. Further classical additions, designed by Smith of Warwick, followed in the 18th century, with the result that the interior of the house is a pleasantly confusing muddle. It has certainly known the great and the good (and bad), including two of Queen Victoria's Prime Ministers, Lords Melbourne and Palmerston, and Lady Caroline Lamb, mistress of Lord Byron, who was banished here before her separation from her husband. They would still recognize much of the furniture and many of the pictures, include *Stuart Courtiers* by Lely and royal portraits by Kneller.

Melbourne's greatest glory is the Versailles-inspired garden laid out with advice from the royal gardeners, London and Wise. This rare survival was begun in 1704 with 'terraces, sloops, verges and fleets of steps' running down to the lake. The delicate wrought-iron arbour, the Birdcage, has gilded leaves rambling over its filigree dome, and suns, moons and flowers decorating its walls.

The house viewed from the Birdcage arbour, made in wrought iron around 1710 by Robert Bakewell of Derby

PENRHYN CASTLE
Gwynedd

3 miles (5km) east of Bangor | Open daily (except Tuesdays) spring to autumn | Tel: 01248 353084 | **www.nationaltrust.org.uk**

Erected in 1819–35 in pink sandstone, this part of
the castle includes the staff quarters and stables

The Grand Staircase was designed by Thomas Hopper
and built between 1820 and 1837 in neo-Norman style

This vast 19th-century neo-Norman castle is situated in some of Wales' most picturesque countryside. Building a vast Victorian mansion in the style of a Norman castle is not unheard of, but what makes Penrhyn Castle so unusual is that, whereas most structures are simply a facade concealing a comfortable range of family rooms, here the theme continues throughout the interior. The castle was built between 1820 and 1845 on the site of a medieval, fortified manor house – and a spiral staircase from the original structure can still be seen.

Thomas Hopper was the bold architect who created this imaginatively forbidding fantasy structure for George Dawkins Pennant, a local slate-quarry owner, whose family made their fortune from Welsh slate and Jamaican sugar.

Hopper's commission also included the suitable fitting out of the interiors of the castle with panelling, plasterwork and furniture. Most of the furniture is 19th-century 'Norman' style, and includes a slate bed weighing over a ton (made for Queen Victoria when she visited in 1859), and a brass bed made especially for Edward VII at the then enormous cost of £600.

The most notable of the rooms includes the Great Hall, which is heated by the Roman hypocaust method of underfloor hot air, the wonderful library with its heavily decorated ceiling and the dining room, covered with neo-Norman decoration. The grand staircase is quite startling in both its proportions – three full storeys high – and its cathedral-like structure of lofty arches, carved stonework and stained glass.

There is an Industrial Railway Museum in the courtyard, a model railway museum and a doll museum; and the whole ensemble is set in 40 acres (16ha) of beautiful grounds between Snowdonia and the Menai Strait, overlooking the North Wales coast.

The heart of the home: the kitchen at Penrhyn Castle is fitted with a gas stove under the arch-shaped windows. A variety of copper pans and a large kettle give an idea of the scale of the catering operation required when the castle was fully occupied

PLAS MAWR Conwy

In the centre of Conwy | Open selected days March to October | Tel: 01492 580167 | www.conwy.com/plasmawr.html

On the north coast of Wales, within the walled medieval town of Conwy, is this architectural gem. Built between 1576 and 1585 for Robert Wynn (or Wynne), a local merchant, Plas Mawr (its name means 'Great Hall') is regarded as the finest surviving Elizabethan town house in Great Britain.

After travelling in Europe, Wynn returned to Conwy, where he married and began building Plas Mawr. Sadly, his wife died the year after the work was completed, but he married again, at the age of sixty-six, and the couple had seven children in just six years. Wynn, who rose to take his place among local gentry, went on in 1589 to become Member of Parliament for Caernarfon.

Plas Mawr, which Wynn described as a 'worthy, plentiful house' is a striking sight in the narrow streets at the centre of Conwy, with its stepped gables, gatehouse and lookout tower, its walls rendered in lime. The interior is finely furnished in the authentic period style (based on a 1665 inventory of the house contents): many of the pieces are indeed original to the house. The house is noted for its fine ornamental plasterwork and the colourful overmantel in the hall.

The house has been restored to its original appearance with help from Cadw (the historic environment service of the Welsh Assembly Government), which recently helped restore the Tudor gardens to mark the 400th anniversary of Wynn's death. These retain many of the original features, including the high garden walls, the division into upper and lower terraces and the original stone-lined drains (which still work).

Plas Mawr is a fascinating example of a prosperous age, and truly reflects the taste and ambition of this north Wales gentleman during the reign of Elizabeth I.

The Elizabethan town house of Plas Mawr is a surprising find in the streets of Conwy

PLAS NEWYDD Gwynedd

It would be hard to find a more delightful location for a grand house such as this than on the sheltered east side of Anglesey, with views across the Menai Strait to the mountains of Snowdonia. There has been a house on the site since the 14th century, but any evidence of it was swept away in the early 1800s by James Wyatt when he redesigned the house with both Gothic and neo-Classical features.

Plas Newydd was the home of the Marquesses of Anglesey until 1976, when it was passed to the care of the National Trust. There are reminders in the house of the family, including the 1st Marquess of Anglesey, who commanded Wellington's cavalry at Waterloo, losing a leg in the last moments of the battle. A collection of uniforms and headdresses continues the military theme.

An early morning view of the east front of Plas Newydd

In the 1930s, the 6th Marquess commissioned Rex Whistler to paint a huge mural in the dining room. The artist's largest work ever, it was completed just before the outbreak of World War II, during which he lost his life. The mural, featuring Whistler himself as a gardener, now forms the centrepiece of an exhibition of his work.

PLAS YN RHIW Gwynedd

4½ miles (7km) north east of Aberdaron | Open selected afternoons March to October | Tel: 01758 780219 | **www.nationaltrust.org.uk**

Hell's Mouth Bay (Porth Neigwl in Welsh), named for its reputation as a graveyard for sailing ships, is hardly an inviting address and yet this small and delightful manor house is to be found on the west shore of the bay.

Dating back to the medieval period and predominantly Tudor, Plas yn Rhiw was extended in the 1630s and again in the 18th and 19th centuries. Later the house fell into a sad state of disrepair and stood empty for some years, but thankfully this little gem was rescued and restored by the three Keating sisters, who bought it in 1938. The sisters gave the property to the National Trust in 1949, but they remained in the house until the death of the last sister in 1981.

The 50 acres (20ha) of gardens and grounds stretching down to the shoreline were also reclaimed and replanted with rhododendrons, azaleas and some sub-tropical shrubs. Box hedges and grass paths divide the gardens and a stream and waterfall tumble down towards the bay; behind the house is a snowdrop wood.

The house and grounds are at the centre of an estate that extends for a further 416 acres (168ha) and includes traditional Welsh cottages, an old windmill and the area known as Mynydd y Craig – a remote and dramatic stretch of Lleyn Peninsula coastline.

The Keating sisters bought Plas yn Rhiw in 1938 and restored it to a charming and simple home

RAGLEY HALL Warwickshire

Colourful friezes decorate the walls of Ragley Hall's South Staircase

Ragley Hall was merely a shell when the Seymour family inherited it, and they did not get around to filling it in until 1750, when James Gibbs designed the baroque plaster decoration with Britannia as its centrepiece in the Great Hall. Thirty years later, James Wyatt redesigned the Red Saloon and the two Mauve Rooms in anticipation of a visit by George III. He also built the stately portico and the stable block.

Architecturally, little has changed since then, partly because many of the later Seymours (who held the title Marquess of Hertford from 1793) did not allow it to distract them from their colourful lives. The 2nd Marchioness caused a scandal through her close friendship with the Prince Regent. The 3rd Marchioness inherited two huge fortunes from men who thought they were her father. Her husband was an avid art collector, a trait shared with their son, who spent his life in great luxury in Paris, and these two men founded the Wallace Collection in Hertford House, London. The next pair of Marquesses worked hard on running the Ragley estate, although the 6th put more effort into hunting and shooting. Incidentally, in 1916, he personally captured the German machine-gun displayed in the North Staircase Hall. He considered his son such a reprobate that he disinherited him, and the house was in a sorry state when it eventually came to Hugh, the 8th Marquess, who spent many years refurbishing it. In 1991 he handed it over to his son, Henry.

Apart from its superb interior decor, Ragley Hall is home to treasures old and new. There are several Old Masters, including van Haarlem's *The Raising of Lazarus* in the Red Saloon. The dining room features royal portraits and a collection of silver.

ROCKINGHAM CASTLE Leicestershire

2 miles (3km) north of Corby | Open selected afternoons April to September | Tel: 01536 770240 | **www.rockinghamcastle.com**

Rockingham Castle stands on a high hill overlooking Rockingham Forest, and was a stronghold in Saxon times. William the Conqueror ordered the building of a castle here in 1066, and it had close royal links for 543 years. Henry VIII had a hunting lodge put up because the castle had fallen into disrepair, and it was the huge, imperious King who leased the castle to Edward Watson in 1544. He spent thirty years converting it into a Tudor home, dividing the Great Hall into separate rooms in the process. It was finally sold by James I for £350 to his grandson, Sir Lewis Watson, in 1619.

Sir Lewis maintained the Watson's good relationship with the Crown, but his wife Eleanor's Parliamentarian links divided the family during the Civil War. Poor Sir Lewis tried to play safe by sending his treasure to his brother-in-law's home, Belvoir Castle, but he was unlucky: Royalists took Belvoir, while Rockingham fell to the Parliamentarians. The badly vandalized castle was returned to Sir Lewis after the war, and its restoration took up the rest of his life, and most of his son's. However, by 1669 it was complete, and much as it is today, apart from some remodelling and the addition of a tower in 1838.

An aerial view of Rockingham Castle shows its impressive self-contained layout

Visitors come in via the Servant's Hall, where some of the Norman stonework remains, and then pass along the charming cobbled 'street', once the centre of life for the self-sufficient community of the castle. The 17th-century Long Gallery is possibly the finest room in the house, with its Chippendale furniture, and more fine paintings. Here large parties were held in the 19th century and Charles Dickens produced and acted in several of his own plays.

SHIPTON HALL Shropshire

Shipton Hall was built around 1587 by Richard Lutwyche to replace a much older black and white timbered house, which was destroyed by a fire earlier in the 16th century. Richard Lutwyche lived at a neighbouring manor, Lutwyche Hall, and it is said that he gave Shipton as a dowry when his daughter Elizabeth married Thomas Mytton. Shipton remained in the Mytton family for the next 300 years.

The house has been described as 'an exquisite specimen of Elizabethan architecure set in a quaint old-fashioned garden, the whole forming a picture which, as regards both form and colour, satisfies the artistic sense of even the most fastidious.'

Externally, the mellow golden stone of the Hall and its attendant Georgian Stable Block blends in perfectly with the beautiful countryside of Shropshire's Corvedale. Inside the house there is an interesting combination of elegant Georgian rococo decor with some beautiful Tudor panelling and timberwork. The latter gives insight into how the house was constructed and illustrates the transition from black and white timbers to stone and brick-built houses. Many of the medieval timbers from the older manor house and some of the doors still survive in Shipton today.

Items of particular interest inside the house are the plasterwork of the ceilings and chimneypieces, some of which are the work of Thomas F Pritchard. The panelling of the Queen's Room and the old solar, and the glazing of the windows – many of which retain the original leaded diamond panes – date from the 16th and 17th centuries.

Elizabethan Shipton Hall is built from mellow Shropshire stone

STOKESAY COURT

5 miles (8km) north west of Ludlow | Open April to December for pre-booked tours | Tel: 01584 856238 | **www.stokesaycourt.co.uk**

Set within extensive grounds in the rolling South Shropshire countryside, Stokesay Court is a magnificent late-Victorian mansion with Jacobean-style facade, built for John Derby-Allcroft, a wealthy entrepreneur, philanthropist and evangelical Christian who had made a vast fortune from the manufacture of gloves.

Allcroft had bought the Stokesay Castle estate in the late 1860s from the Earl of Craven and set about restoring the 13th-century fortified manor house as a site of historic interest. By the time Stokesay Court was completed in 1892, it was at the cutting edge of new technology and design and was one of the first houses in England to be built with integral electric light. Its architect, Thomas Harris, was better known as an industrial rather than a domestic architect and this can be seen in much of the infrastructure of the building.

The house has three wings, laid out around a central block; a bachelors' or gentlemen's wing to the west, a ladies' wing opposite facing the garden, and a servants' wing in between. During World War I the house was used as an auxiliary military hospital for convalescent soldiers; during World War II it became a Western Command Junior Leaders' School and was home to some boys from Lancing College for a year. Throughout this time the family remained living at Stokesay and the house has survived intact and remarkably untouched to this day.

In the summer of 2006, Stokesay Court was a primary location for the film adaptation of Ian McEwan's haunting novel *Atonement*, starring Keira Knightley and James McAvoy. Guided tours giving a behind-the-scenes look at the rooms used in the adaptation are extremely popular.

The Great Hall (right) and the wisteria-clad walls of the east view of Stokesay Court (top)

Home to the Morgans for over 500 years, Tredegar provided much of the wealth that enabled commercial and industrial development to take place in Newport in the 18th and 19th centuries. The Morgan family were generous benefactors to the community, giving land for the Royal Gwent Hospital, and helping to encourage recreation and educational facilities in the area.

The Morgans, although they claim descent from the great princely families of Wales, are likely to have attained gentry status only in the early Tudor period, when they constructed a grand house to reflect their new social position. Tredegar was clearly a substantial house, but was unlikely to satisfy the ambitions of the greatest family in the district indefinitely. In 1645, after the Battle of Naseby, Charles I, his retinue and two troops of horse spent the night at Tredegar, courtesy of Sir William Morgan, and it was his grandson, another William, who created the house that we see today. It consisted of two wings at right-angles to each other, forming a hollow square with the old medieval hall and the later offices.

Tredegar was a wonder of Wales in the late 17th century, and symbolized the Morgan's power and influence for the following 250 years. The family's wealth increased, enabling Sir William to live a short but rich life, to marry a daughter of the 2nd Duke of Devonshire, and to be created a Knight of the Bath in 1725. The estates passed to his niece, Jane, and she married Sir Charles Gould, an astute lawyer, who changed his name to Gould Morgan and invested the Tredegar fortunes in industrial and financial projects. It was for loyalty to Disraeli that Sir Charles Morgan was created 1st Baron Tredegar in 1859. He was succeeded by one of the most colourful Morgans, Godfrey, who had survived the Charge of the Light Brigade. A nephew,

Elegant sculpture and red hot pokers in the formal walled gardens of Tredegar House

Courtenay, succeeded in 1913, and he and his son, Evan, the last Morgan to live at Tredegar, indulged an extravagant life-style that was to lead John Morgan to sell the estate in 1951 to meet death duties. After more than twenty years as a school, the house, stables, home farm, gardens and 90 acres (36ha) of parkland were purchased by Newport Borough Council.

In 1911 there were twenty-two indoor servants at Tredegar, and the house is fortunate in having a series of well-appointed rooms that give a clear idea of how a great house worked. The kitchen, with its roasting range and spit, is fascinating.

WARWICK CASTLE Warwickshire

In the centre of Warwick | Open every day except Christmas | Tel: 0871 265 2000 | www.warwick-castle.co.uk

You can easily see why the Normans built a castle on this site in 1068: the high escarpment offers a superb view of the surrounding countryside, and one side is formed by the cliff over the banks of the River Avon. The motte and bailey fortress was put under the control of Henry de Newburgh, who was to become the 1st Earl of Warwick. Traces of the motte (or mound) survive today, and it has been restored, but most of the structure today was built in the 14th century by Thomas de Beauchamp and his son of the same name. Funding was provided by Thomas's booty from the Hundred Years' War.

Thomas and his son constructed the north curtain wall with its pair of towers, and the main gatehouse, through which visitors enter today. In the gatehouse, an exhibition called the 'Kingmaker attraction' explains the behind-the-scenes action that took place prior to the Battle of Barnet – a battle that the Earl of Warwick himself fought in. The Beauchamps' masterpiece was Caesar's Tower, a 150 feet- (46m-) high wall tower with an unusual double parapet. There was once a jail on this site used to hold prisoners for short periods of time before they were transferred to other establishments.

A walk on the ramparts between Clarence Tower and Guy's Tower, gives a strong feeling of what it was like to defend this fortress from attackers. You also get a good view of River Island and the tranquil gardens. These cover 60 acres (24ha) and were landscaped by 'Capability' Brown. Peacocks roam contentedly through the grounds, which feature a woodland garden. Another attraction is the restored Victorian Rose Garden, created by Robert Marnock.

The sun warms the stone of the impressive Norman east front of Warwick Castle

WESTON PARK Shropshire

The well-kept exterior of Weston Park seen from the manicured plane tree lawn

Weston Park, completed in 1617, was built on the site of an earlier medieval manor house, and since that time it has been the family seat of the Earls of Bradford. Additions and alterations in the intervening years have created an extensive collection of buildings, in a number of different styles. In recent years, however, the present owners, the Earl and Countess of Bradford, have undone many of the Victorian alterations to restore the house and grounds to a condition nearer to the original 17th-century plan.

The interior is cool, airy and sumptuously appointed, with period furniture and art treasures collected by the family over the centuries: important paintings include works by Stubbs, Constable and Van Dyck. Displayed in the entrance hall are paintings that reflect the 3rd Earl's passion for horses, while the dominant feature of the adjacent Marble Hall is its floor with contrasting squares of white marble and black slate. The Tapestry Room, by contrast, is a symphony of pinks, its walls draped with beautiful tapestries woven at the famous Gobelin factory in Paris. They feature mythological scenes after the styles of Reubens and Watteau. The drawing room holds a series of family portraits, including one of Lady Wilbraham by Sir Peter Lely.

A pair of salons created from a former courtyard are now used as galleries for an impressive display of landscape, genre and portrait paintings. The breakfast room is another that has been redesigned to set off pictures – in this case a collection of the best smaller portraits, including a painting of Sir George Carew by Holbein. Of the bedrooms, one of particular interest is the elegant Tent Room, which has been sumptuously redecorated in the French style, with a tented ceiling and walls hung with silk drapes.

1	**Adlington Hall** Cheshire	148
2	**Alnwick Castle** Northumberland	149
3	**Arley Hall** Cheshire	150
4	**Bamburgh Castle** Northumberland	151
5	**Burton Agnes Hall** Yorkshire	152
6	**Burton Constable Hall** Yorkshire	154
7	**Capesthorne Hall** Cheshire	155
8	**Castle Howard** Yorkshire	156
9	**Chillingham Castle** Northumberland	157
10	**Chipchase Castle** Northumberland	158
11	**Cragside** Northumberland	159
12	**Dalemain** Cumbria	160
13	**Dorfold Hall** Cheshire	161
14	**Fairfax House** Yorkshire	162
15	**Gawsworth Hall** Cheshire	163
16	**Harewood House** Yorkshire	164
17	**Hoghton Tower** Lancashire	166
18	**Holker Hall** Cumbria	167
19	**Hutton-in-the-Forest** Cumbria	169
20	**Kiplin Hall** Yorkshire	170
21	**Leighton Hall** Lancashire	171
22	**Levens Hall** Cumbria	172
23	**Meols Hall** Lancashire	174
24	**Mirehouse** Cumbria	175
25	**Muncaster Castle** Cumbria	176
26	**Newby Hall** Yorkshire	177
27	**Peover Hall** Cheshire	178
28	**Preston Tower** Northumberland	179
29	**Raby Castle** County Durham	180
30	**Ripley Castle** Yorkshire	181
31	**Rode Hall** Cheshire	182
32	**Rokeby Park** County Durham	183
33	**Rydal Mount** Cumbria	184
34	**Seaton Delaval Hall** Northumberland	185
35	**Sizergh Castle** Cumbria	186
36	**Sledmere House** Yorkshire	188
37	**Stockeld Park** Yorkshire	189
38	**Wallington** Northumberland	190

NORTHERN ENGLAND | 4

A feature of the unique rugged landscape of this region, pele towers, needed for security in the wild lands of the north, became part of comfortable houses in more settled times – as at Levens Hall, a gorgeous Elizabethan mansion full of ghosts that, understandably, refuse to leave it. The same is true of Muncaster Castle, with its superlative views over Eskdale, while Raby Castle bares its savage teeth in County Durham. Further south, civilized grandeur peaks in the baroque magnificence of Castle Howard and the Georgian stylishness of Harewood House. Newby Hall is a Wren-style dream in red brick. Gillow furniture and birds of prey distinguish Leighton Hall. Charlotte Brontë knew Norton Conyers and Wordsworth lived at Rydal Mount. Browsholme Hall belongs to the hereditary Bowbearers of the Forest of Bowland, Sledmere House takes its charm from generations of Sykeses, while Leghs have resided at Adlington Hall through seven centuries.

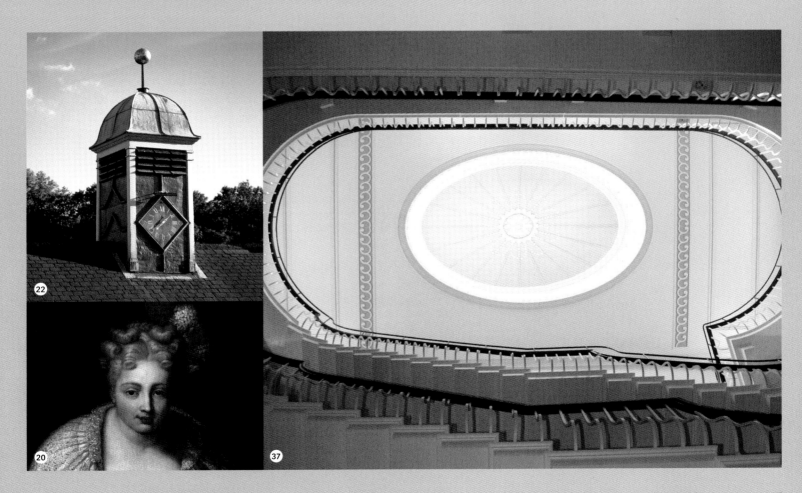

ADLINGTON HALL Cheshire

4 miles (6km) north of Macclesfield | Open selected days July and August; guided groups by arrangement | Tel: 01625 827595 | **www.adlingtonhall.com**

Adlington Hall is built on the site of a hunting lodge, around a quadrangle. It was once surrounded by a moat. Since the beginning of the 14th century Adlington has been owned by the Legh family, whose ancestors include King Stephen and one Gilbert de Venables, who was knighted by William the Conqueror on the battlefield at Hastings.

The Great Hall was built by Thomas Legh at the end of the 15th century, first in timber, then refaced in brick and stone. The rest of the house was added in 1581, by another Thomas Legh – mostly in the half-timbered style. The north front was rebuilt by yet another Thomas Legh in about 1670. Successive owners have made further additions, reflecting the changing tastes of successive generations, and the result is an intriguing amalgam of architectural styles.

Adlington's glory is the Great Hall – the first impression one of space. The roof-ridge is fully 38 feet (12m) high – a splendid example of the hammer-beam style, which is richly embellished with mouldings and carvings. Two oak trees support the east end of the hall, all that now remains of the original hunting lodge. In the dining room, the decoration is provided mostly by family portraits. The walls of the beautifully proportioned drawing room are divided into panels by fluted Corinthian columns. Above the doors and the marble fireplace are carved festoons of fruit and leaves. A minstrels' gallery provides an alternative view down into the Great Hall.

The gardens were landscaped in the style that 'Capability' Brown had popularized. Visitors can see a Temple to Diana and take a stroll along the Yew Walk and Lime Avenue.

The black-and-white wing of Adlington Hall has been carefully restored to its former glory

ALNWICK CASTLE Northumberland

In Alnwick | Open daily March to October | Tel: 01665 510777 or 01665 511100 (24-hour information) | www.alnwickcastle.com

'When the Duke of Northumberland is willing to receive visits from the neighbouring gentry,' read an early 19th-century notice at Alnwick, 'a flag is hung upon the highest turret as a signal that he may be approached'. In these more democratic days, visiting times are more regular, but the castle still demonstrates the tremendous aristocratic pride, wealth, power and influence of the Percy family. They came over with William the Conqueror, but the line can be traced back further, to the Emperor Charlemagne's grandmother.

Alnwick came to the Percys in 1309, and it has remained one of their principal homes – along with Syon House near London. Yet it was not the Percy family who founded and built the first castle at Alnwick. Another of the Conqueror's companions, his standard-bearer Gilbert Tyson, was the first Norman to own the site, but forfeited it after rebellion against the King in 1095. It passed to Yvo de Vescy the following year, and it was he who founded the castle we see today. His son-in-law completed the main form of the castle before his death in 1147.

It must have been an intimidating sight in the Middle Ages, with its circular shell keep, studded with fearsome towers, and the outer wall enclosing the two baileys, also bristling with bastions. Alnwick has kept its shape through more than 800 years, though inevitably there have been alterations, repairs, renewals and, certainly inside, wholesale transformations. It might not have been so, however, for, after the barons revolted against King John in 1212, among them Eustace de Vescy, the king ordered its total destruction. Fortunately it survived both that threat and burning by Alexander, King of

The turrets of Alnwick Castle seen from the Lion Bridge, where the Percy's crest, a lion, stands guard

Scotland, as well as a siege by Prince Edward after John de Vescy had backed the rebel side in the Battle of Evesham.

'Capability' Brown was called in by the 1st Duke to tame the rugged Northumberland scenery into the beautiful sweeps of grass and trees that provide Alnwick's fine, though perhaps unauthentic, setting. The Duke was also responsible for Robert Adam's Brizlee Tower of 1781, 2 miles (3km) away. In the Gothic style, it is crowned with a large cast-iron basket in which to light a beacon for ducal festivals. Adam's brother John designed the Lion Bridge in 1773, a medieval vision of battlements and lookouts, with the Percy's crest, a statant lion, guarding its parapet, a proud symbol of this noblest of families.

ARLEY HALL Cheshire

4½ miles (7km) north of Northwich | Open selected afternoons April to October | Tel: 01565 777353 | **www.arleyhallandgardens.com**

A colourful show in the gardens of Arley Hall

The Arley estate has been in the Egerton-Warburton family since the 15th century, though the Hall itself is actually a Victorian edifice. It replaced an 18th-century house, which was itself built onto an earlier timber-framed house. It was Rowland Egerton-Warburton who, in 1832, approved the plans for the building we see today, which is a symmetrical, many-windowed design every bit as conservative as its then owner. The

architect was a local man, George Latham of Nantwich.

The entrance to the Hall is through a red-brick gatehouse topped with a wooden clock tower, part of a group of outbuildings that includes a handsome cruck-framed barn dating back to the family's first occupancy of the estate. The barn now offers visitors refreshments and light meals served in authentically antique surroundings.

The sturdy facade of the Hall itself is enlivened by diamond-shaped patterns

in the brickwork, heraldic beasts and ornamental chimneys that have been given an anachronistic 'barley-sugar' twist. The few genuine Jacobean details, salvaged from older houses, cannot disguise the fact that Arley Hall represents both a style and a self-confidence that typify the Victorian era.

While Arley Hall boasts few paintings of note, the spacious rooms, with their high ceilings, are full of fine craftsmanship – particularly voluminous fireplaces, wood panelling and plaster work. The wooden bookcases in the library reveal something of a taste for Gothic eccentricity. The drawing room provides an intimate space for some of the family's treasured possessions, while the dining room contains virginals dating back to 1675. Throughout the house are a number of long-case clocks and some fine porcelain.

Having invested in the solid virtues of bricks and mortar, the Hall's founder next sought to cater for his family's spiritual welfare. Architect Anthony Salvin was called in to create a private chapel, largely in the Decorated Gothic style that became so popular during Victoria's reign. But Rowland Egerton-Warburton's energies extended far beyond the Arley estate, and he took it upon himself to both build and repair buildings in some of the nearby villages.

The 12 acres (5ha) of gardens are a special delight. Originally laid out by Rowland Egerton-Warburton while the Hall itself was under construction, they have been brought to their present condition through the attentions of Lady Ashbrook, the mother of the present owner. There are many garden styles to enjoy, including a splendid double herbaceous border, yew hedges, topiary, a walled garden, a herb garden and a colourful collection of more than 200 varieties of rhododendrons. An avenue of clipped *Quercus ilex* contrasts with the grove and its informal woodland walks.

BAMBURGH CASTLE Northumberland

14 miles (22km) north of Alnwick | Open daily February to November; weekends November to February | Tel: 01668 214515 | www.bamburghcastle.com

If you want a castle that really looks like a castle, Bamburgh's the place. Its setting is superb, and it crouches ferociously on its fearsome crag like a whole medieval town. Beyond it are only the empty dunes and cold North Sea, with Holy Island, once under the castle's protection, on the horizon. This outcrop of basalt has been defended since the Iron Age. After the departure of the Romans, Bamburgh was a royal Saxon capital and was sacked by the Vikings. It fell easily to William the Conqueror, but with its new Norman keep and walls was absolutely impregnable until, in 1464, Edward IV's new artillery made it the first castle ever to be shelled into submission. Thereafter Bamburgh, with its walls broken and its roof shattered, succumbed to the elements.

The Forster family held the castle from the reign of James I until the early 18th century, when it passed to Lord Crewe, Bishop of Durham. He left it as part of a charitable trust and it was sold in 1894 to the 1st Lord Armstrong, whose family still owns it. It was repaired and restored in the 18th century, but in the 19th century it was extensively reconstructed in turn-of-the century Gothic.

The state rooms include the panelled Great Hall, with an impressive hammer-beam roof and a musicians' gallery. The Hall houses an excellent display of armour from the Tower of London's Royal Armoury collection.

In the 18th century Dr John Sharp restored the castle and ran a remarkable charity under the terms of Lord Crewe's will. There was a free school, an infirmary, a free lending library for the use of the poor, and a mill where corn was ground and sold very cheaply. Dr Sharp also set up one of the first coastguard and lifeboat stations in the country, and provided homes for shipwrecked sailors.

Bamburgh Castle has an interesting history and is impressively warlike, both inside and out

BURTON AGNES HALL Yorkshire

The same family has owned this property since Roger de Stuteville built a manor house here in 1173. The builder of the Elizabethan mansion was Sir Henry Griffith, who employed Robert Smithson, master mason to Queen Elizabeth, as his architect. Uniquely, his plans have been preserved, revealing not only the unity of the design but also how little has been changed. In the 17th century the property passed to Sir Matthew Boynton, a Royalist who changed sides and was appointed Governor of Scarborough Castle by Cromwell. His son rebelled in favour of the King and was killed in 1651 in the advance of the Royalist army from Scotland. An 18th-century stepfather nearly ruined the family. 'Handsome Jack' married the widow of the 6th Baronet, spent a fortune and brought her sons up 'in every sort of vice'. Later generations proved more responsible and extensively restored this delightful house.

A turreted early 17th-century gatehouse is a foretaste of the glories to come. The perfect symmetry of the red-brick mansion, three storeys high, with two square and two compass bays, is preserved by having the entrance door at the side of one of the bays. A profusion of biblical, allegorical and mythological figures are carved into the remarkable Elizabethan screen and massive alabaster chimneypiece, almost the height of the wall in the Great Hall. The Red Drawing Room is an incredible example of brilliantly painted and gilded Elizabethan panelling with another outstanding carved chimneypiece depicting the Dance of Death. The plasterwork ceilings, intricate carvings and panelling and superb collection of family portraits make this a house to remember.

Burton Agnes has a ghost – of Anne, youngest daughter of Sir Henry Griffin. Fatally wounded by robbers, Anne declared she could never rest unless part of her remained at Burton Agnes. When they ignored her wishes and buried her in the churchyard, her ghost walked until her family fulfilled their promise and moved her to the site – and it walks again if ever she is disturbed.

Beautifully kept grounds and charmingly furnished rooms characterize Burton Agnes Hall

BURTON CONSTABLE HALL East Yorkshire

There has been a building on this site since at least the Middle Ages and a medieval manor house survives as part of the present building, comprising the north wing and its tower with projecting staircase turret. In the later 1560s Sir John Constable added the Great Hall and another tower and wing to harmonize with the existing structures. The west front with its gallery was added shortly afterwards. Much of the building described in a survey of 1578 as 'one goodly manor house of aintient building' (sic) still exists, concealed behind later work. Until the 18th century a turreted gatehouse and two courtyards protected the house from the public road to the east. As it stands today, however, the house owes most to a sensitive remodelling that took place under William Constable in the late 18th century. While retaining most of the original exterior, he employed some of the most illustrious craftsmen of the day to transform the interior into a series of elegant Georgian rooms. Robert Adam, James Wyatt and John Carr all contributed designs for the interior alterations, Timothy Lightoler added the new stable block and Thomas Atkinson the orangery.

The exterior of the house is graceful and imposing: three storeys high, built of red brick, with stone mullioned and oriel windows and castellated towers, it has a pleasing symmetry. The focal point of the east facade is the pillared entrance, surmounted by a pediment displaying the family coat of arms. Thomas Chippendale supplied the chairs, sofas, firescreens and side tables in the ballroom, but John Lowry, a former estate apprentice, who went on to set up business in London, was responsible for the superb nine-piece pedestal table and chairs in the dining room.

Elegant furnishings and a collection of portraits in the drawing room of Burton Constable Hall

CAPESTHORNE HALL Cheshire

4½ miles (7km) west of Macclesfield | Open selected days April to October | Tel: 01625 861221 | www.capesthorne.com

The house is announced from a distance by smoke-blackened towers, domes and pinnacles rising up from the Cheshire countryside. The entrance hall leads immediately into the Sculpture Gallery, where visitors can admire Capesthorne's important collection of classical marbles and later busts. In the Saloon it is easy to imagine the dances that were held here. The chairs and sofas were made in Ceylon, now Sri Lanka.

The drawing room is one of many rooms reconstructed by Anthony Salvin after a disastrous fire in 1861. The twin fireplaces, brought here from the family's town house in Belgravia, were made in 1789 and are splendid examples of Coade stone. Through the drawing room is the Bromley Staircase, lined with portraits of the Bromley family. Upstairs, outside the Dorothy Davenport Room, is a fascinating collection of watercolours painted in the 1830s by James Johnson and Edward Blore. Further on is a family tree that traces their unbroken descent from the Norman Conquest.

In the Queen Anne Room a monumental fireplace displays the family arms, portrait busts, reliefs of Roman emperors and classical priests. The Coalport china displayed in the two alcoves inspired the apple-green walls and contemporary fabric.

Capesthorne's park has a delightful trio of lakes, formed by damming a nearby stream, around which are shady walks and scenic views back towards the house. A mirror trout of over 33lbs (150kg), taken in 1983 by a lucky angler, proved to be a record catch for Cheshire. In summer the water surface is brightened by floating blooms of the yellow water-lily. There are lovely walks at any season of the year, though in springtime they are enhanced by colourful profusions of bluebells and rhododendrons.

The distinctive Jacobean style house with its delightful gardens and lakes is set in over 100 acres of parkland

CASTLE HOWARD Yorkshire

12 miles (19km) north of York | Open daily March to October; and pre-Christmas period | Tel: 01653 648640 | **www.castlehoward.co.uk**

Above and top: The dome and roof statues of Castle Howard create a particularly romantic silhouette

The full magnificence of Castle Howard is best appreciated from the south, where it is viewed in dramatic outline against the horizon. The sheer scale of the Grand Staircase and the vast, echoing rooms are imposing, and there is no denying the splendour of the bedrooms and dressing rooms that follow. Four-poster beds of every conceivable design contrive to reduce the height of the ceilings. Queen Victoria slept in the 18th-century bed with its unusual circular top, which dominates the Castle Howard Dressing Room. On the occasion of her visit in 1850, gas was first installed in the castle, and her entrance was heralded with a display of flames spelling out 'God Save the Queen' on the hall balcony.

A corridor has been turned from a utilitarian necessity into a novel Antique Passage, where antiquities from the 4th Earl's collections are displayed. The Great Hall is a triumph of Vanbrugh's art on an altogether different scale. Its vastness is accentuated by the heavy pillars that draw the eye upwards to the wrought-iron balcony of the gallery and the dizzying height of the dome 70 feet (21m) above. The plunging horses and arresting figure of Phaeton, tumbling from Apollo's chariot, are an entirely appropriate subject for the ceiling of the dome. By comparison with such monumental grandeur, the rest of the house seems positively domestic, but a series of glittering state rooms provide the setting for a collection of fabulous paintings.

Brideshead Revisited, Evelyn Waugh's story of love and loss, was filmed at Castle Howard in 1981 and a more perfect location for the house whose spirit permeates the book would be hard to imagine.

CHILLINGHAM CASTLE Northumberland

15 miles (24km) north of Alnwick | Open selected afternoons April to October | Tel: 01668 215359 | **www.chillingham-castle.com**

Sir Walter Scott may have used Chillingham as his model for Osbaldistone Hall in *Rob Roy*, for this impressive open square of a castle, with its four great corner towers, has been famous in the borders for centuries. Held by the Grey family since they took it by force in 1245, it remains the home of their line to this day, though soldiers burned the castle's north wing in the 1940s, and rot ravaged the place until Sir Humphrey Wakefield, who married into the Grey family, began its rescue and restoration in the 1980s.

The restoration work has revealed more of the building's history – including a bundle of Tudor documents hidden in a walled-up fireplace. Such discoveries help to put the long history of the Grey family into perspective. Only ten years after the original tower was captured they entertained Henry III at Chillingham, and Edward I followed in 1298. By that time the castle had taken on much of the appearance we see today, for Sir Thomas Grey was allowed to 'crenellate' or fortify it in 1344. A moat gave added protection and made the dungeons, with their sinister oubliette, in which prisoners were thrown and forgotten, even more dank and alarming than they are today. As one of the most important families in the north – often in rivalry with the Percys at nearby Alnwick – they played an important role in helping to keep the Scots from causing trouble. The armoured effigy of one, Sir Ralph, who died in 1443, is found on a magnificent tomb in the church at the castle's gates.

Georgian additions were made in 1753 and, after a fire in 1803, new state apartments were built in the East Range, which suffered badly when the house was unoccupied. George IV's architect from Windsor Castle, Wyatville, was called in for further modifications by Charles Grey, 5th Earl of Tankerville; this title was originally acquired by one Sir Ralph Grey of Chillingham in 1409, when he stormed the castle of Tancaville in Normandy. The 5th Earl was responsible for importing the two great marble chimneypieces in the Great Hall from the magnificent Wanstead House in Essex, built by architect Colen Campbell in 1720.

Outside, grass had been brought right up to the castle walls in the 18th century – the moat is now a huge tunnel under the south lawn. Wyatville added long avenues of trees and designed a new formal garden on the site of the medieval tournament ground. Its elaborate hedges and plantings survived until the 1930s, when it rapidly became overgrown and unrecognizable. It has recently been rescued from its near-desolation and now forms a replica of an Elizabethan garden, well suited to the grandeur of one of the north's most important castles.

Older even than the castle, the 1,000 acre- (405ha-) park at Chillingham has been walled since 1220. Uncultivated for more than 650 years, it is still medieval in its atmosphere.

Chillingham Castle is surrounded by clipped hedges and formal gardens

CHIPCHASE CASTLE Northumberland

2 miles (3km) south east of Wark-on-Tyne | Open afternoons in June and at other times by arrangement | Tel: 01434 230203 | www.chipchasecastle.com

If you look north from the line of Hadrian's Wall you can see Chipchase Castle, high on its plateau above the North Tyne. It is a magical mix of medieval, Jacobean and Georgian, reflecting both the turbulent history of the area and the vicissitudes of its ownership. Like many Northumbrian houses, it began life as a defensive pele tower against the Scots' frequent raids – and against the neighbours and authorities, too, for the Heron family, who owned Chipchase from 1348, were a quarrelsome lot.

How long the tower stood alone is unclear, but by 1541 a stone manor house was joined to it. It was from here that the Herons, as Keepers of Tyndale, set out on Scottish raids, sometimes in defiance of their overlords. The entire history of the family seems to have consisted of skirmish, capture and bloodshed. In 1537 John Heron was accused of murder, but was later pardoned. His son, Sir George, was himself killed by the Scots at Carter Bar. The Heron estates, which were considerable, were inherited by Cuthbert Heron in 1591 when he was only six. Its E-shaped south-east front makes it one of the north's best buildings of its time, with its two great bow windows – Victorian restorations, but very much in keeping – and the fanciful cresting over the porch tower.

Yet within sixty years of Cuthbert's confident gesture in building a new home, there was almost nothing left of the Heron fortunes. Mortgages and dowries, as well as the difficult political climate of the 17th century, had taken their toll. The family struggled on at Chipchase until 1727, when they were forced to sell. Ownership changed several times until it came to John Reed.

Reed obviously found the Jacobean house dark and gloomy, for he added sash windows and put false windows on the pele so that the south-west side of the house is symmetrical – if you can make the mental effort to ignore the turrets on the medieval tower. He transformed the interiors at Chipchase, too, with elegant plaster ceilings and fine doorcases, particularly in what is now the billiard room, where there is also a superbly carved wooden overmantle, a survivor from the previous house.

Dark and brooding, Chipchase Castle began life as a defensive pele tower

CRAGSIDE Northumberland

2 miles (3km) North of Rothbury | Open March to October daily except Monday | Tel: 01669 620333 | **www.nationaltrust.org.uk**

Cragside was built as a weekend retreat for the 1st Lord Armstrong, who had two careers, first as a lawyer, then as an inventor, engineer and gunmaker in the Victorian tradition. He founded the company that was to become Vickers Armstrong in later years.

Cragside began modestly, but gradually expanded into a proper country mansion with a wildly picturesque outline, well suited to the rugged wooded hills which surround it. Not surprisingly, Armstrong's scientific bent was put to good use here – Cragside was the earliest house in the world to be lit by hydro-electricity, and the kitchen has a hydraulic service lift and a spit powered from a lake above the house.

The drawing room has a double-storey chimney-piece of Italian marble, and the dining room, in Old English style, is one of the finest Victorian domestic rooms in the country. The library, with its light oak panelling and elaborate ceiling, is attractive, and the study is inviting. In contrast to all this 'Englishness' is the Japanese Room, named after its 19th-century prints, and the Bamboo Room, filled with simulated bamboo furniture.

Right and below: Cragside is full of reminders of the industrial age and Armstrong's love of science

DALEMAIN Cumbria

3 miles (5km) south west of Penrith and M6 Junction 40 | Open selected days April to October | Tel: 01768 486450 | **www.dalemain.com**

Like many of the best houses, Dalemain – situated where the Lake District mountains change to softer rolling countryside – has its secrets. The elegant 18th-century front, built of beautiful pale-rose sandstone, hides a building that stretches back through the centuries to the Saxons, who established one of a chain of small forts here. A Norman pele tower, the oldest surviving part of the house, was standing when Hugh de Morville fled to his brother John, its owner, after being involved in the murder of Thomas à Becket. The Layton family, who held Dalemain from the 13th to the 17th centuries, added the buildings round the courtyard. These include the medieval Great Hall, with its Tudor ceiling, and the Priest's Hiding Chamber, originally reached by climbing the kitchen chimney, but accessed now from the housekeeper's room. The haunted solar holds 'The Luck of Dalemain', a superb wine glass of about 1730 engraved with the Hasell coat of arms.

Lady Anne Clifford, a rich heiress, whose portrait hangs here, left a legacy to her 'secretarie' Sir Edward Hasell, and he used it to buy Dalemain in 1679. Another Edward added the classical Georgian front that transformed the jumble of old buildings, with their unexpected changes of level and winding passages, with a series of fine rooms. The star of the show is the Chinese Drawing Room, with its hand-painted Chinese wallpaper featuring a riot of pheasants, peonies and butterflies. It is complemented by Chinese Chippendale chairs and an English fireplace carved with spirited dragons.

A fascinating nursery comes complete with rocking horse, miniature Noah's Ark, dolls' house and a collection of Dinky cars.

Dalemain House has an impressive Georgian frontage. Inside is a glorious profusion of winding passages

160

DORFOLD HALL Cheshire

Ralph Wilbraham built this handsome Jacobean house to celebrate in brick and stone the success he and his family were enjoying in the legal profession. The main block and the two forecourt lodges are of the same period, dated 1616.

Dorfold Hall may have been the site of the manor of Edwin, the last Saxon Earl of Chester, and a grandson of Lady Godiva, whose place in folklore was secured by one short, but memorable, horse ride.

By the end of the 18th century Dorfold was one of Cheshire's most important hunting centres. The name derives from the Saxon word 'Deofold', indicating a cattle enclosure or deer park.

It is remarkable that Dorfold survived the Civil War. Its second owner, Roger Wilbraham, took the Parliamentarian side, an allegiance that led to the house being plundered by Royalist forces in 1643. After five generations of Wilbrahams, Dorfold was bought by another legal man, James Tomkinson, who planted many of the fine trees in the garden, and added the stables for his two dozen hunters. The house has since been handed down to the Roundell family. Dorfold was the last hall in the district to relinquish the 'open

Delightfully wild and untamed gardens are a pleasant feature of Dorfold Hall

house' hospitality of Georgian times, boasting its own butchery, bakery and brew-house.

The Great Chamber's barrel-vaulted plaster ceiling, executed in 1621, is very special; there are few better examples in England. The original chimneypiece, with its Doric columns and family coat of arms, is still in place, as is the ornate panelling. The chamber offers a suitable setting for a selection of fine 16th- and 17th-century furniture and modern family portraits.

FAIRFAX HOUSE Yorkshire

In Castlegate, York | Open selected days February to December | Tel: 01904 655543 | www.fairfaxhouse.co.uk

In 1759, Charles, Viscount Fairfax of Emley, purchased a house and land at Castlegate, overlooking the River Ouse, for his daughter, Anne, the sole survivor of his nine children. The gift was made to compensate Anne for her disappointment in marriage: at the eleventh hour, when the bridal parties were already assembling in London, he stopped her marriage to William Constable of Burton Constable, on the grounds that the groom was not assiduous enough in his attendance at weekday Mass; Fairfax himself was a devout Catholic. He poured a fortune into building a fine new town house for his daughter but his efforts were in vain. She suffered acute nervous disorders, and tried (unsuccessfully) to find a cure in retreats at Cambrai and in Brussels. Father and daughter occupied the house in Castlegate for eleven winters, but when he died she sold it within a year and returned to spend the last twenty-one years of her life alone at Gilling Castle.

Between 1772 and 1865 Fairfax House changed hands six times. After 1865 it was no longer a private house, first becoming a suite of offices for the York Friendly Societies and then, in 1919, its front first-floor rooms were converted into a ballroom. It was purchased by the York Civic Trust in 1981 and restored to house the Noel Terry Collection of furniture.

The house probably dates from around the 1740s but the exterior was extensively remodelled and the interiors transformed by Fairfax in 1759. The Palladian entrance hallway is a triumph, with a carefully contrived vista of archways enticing the visitor into the flamboyantly decorated public rooms. Attentive to every last detail, Fairfax purchased and demolished the house next door to increase the light to his superb Venetian window on the staircase.

The front of Fairfax House, seen from Castlegate

GAWSWORTH HALL Cheshire

Gawsworth, 2½ miles (4km) South of Macclesfield | Open May to September | Tel: 01260 223456 | www.gawsworthhall.com

A fine example of Cheshire black-and-white architecture, Gawsworth Hall was built in the second half of the 15th century and for many years was the home of the Fitton family. Today it is a peaceful and serene household, giving little hint of its eventful past.

They were known as the 'Fighting Fittons' in those days, and Mary Fitton, 'the wayward maid of Gawsworth', is said to be the 'Dark Lady' of Shakespeare's sonnets. The last professional jester in England, Maggoty Johnson, lived at Gawsworth where he was dancing master to the children, and is buried nearby in 'Maggoty Johnson's Wood'.

Originally the house was built around a quadrangle, but it was reduced in size by Charles Gerard, 2nd Earl of Macclesfield, around the end of the 17th century. Today it has all the charm and character of a medieval house, with fine old timbers and ornate fireplaces, and is filled with comfortable old furniture, paintings, sculpture and armour. The delightful little chapel has beautiful stained glass by Burne-Jones and William Morris, while out in the lovely grounds is a rare survivor – an Elizabethan tilting ground.

A range of seasonal events takes place here, including delightful open-air theatrical productions in summer.

Gawsworth's rose-bedecked black-and-white facade and attractive courtyard

HAREWOOD HOUSE West Yorkshire

From unpromising beginnings (according to the Domesday Book, Harewood belonged to three Saxon chieftains, Tor, Sprot and Grim), the Lascelles family has created a treasure house, employing only the finest craftsmen to build and embellish it.

Lascelles came over to England with William the Conqueror. Later Colonel Francis Lascelles fought for Parliament in the Civil War and went on to become MP for North Riding, beginning a long family tradition of parliamentary service. A fortune derived from sugar plantations in the West Indies enabled his grandson to buy Gawthorpe and Harewood, and his great-grandson, Edwin Lascelles, to realize his dream of building a grand new house on the hill.

Rejecting the first set of plans drawn up by William Chambers, Edwin then commissioned John Carr of York, after the latter had proved himself by building a satisfactory stable block. After entrusting Carr with building the house, a farm and model village, he then referred the plans to the then up-and-coming Scottish architect, Robert Adam. Though Adam changed little of the Palladian exterior of the house, the interior was entirely committed into his care, resulting in a glorious series of state rooms. He determined the prevalence of the classical motif in the decorations, oversaw the delicate and elaborate plasterwork designs and even selected all the carpets. He commissioned Thomas Chippendale, born only a few miles away at Otley, to provide all the furniture and furnishings, a task that he performed with both flair and sympathy. The simple elegance and understated opulence of even his inlaid and gilded pieces are the perfect complement to Adam's room schemes.

The foundation stone was laid in January 1759, but it was not until twelve years later that the house became habitable. The following year, 'Capability' Brown submitted his plans for landscaping the park, creating a 'natural' undulating vista from the house down to the artificial lake. Planting woodland and altering the lie of the land took nine years and cost £6,000, but created an idyllic and supremely English setting for this gem of a country house.

The first glimpse of Harewood House is intimidating, soaring above the level parkland, with neither buildings nor trees to soften the approach. Visitors cannot fail to be impressed by the sheer size and magnificence of the north facade. The entrance is dominated by a classical pediment and pillars. The entrance hall itself is equally stern and cold, its walls and ceilings covered with roundels depicting stories from classical myths: even the alabaster figure of Adam, by Jacob Epstein, which stands sentinel here, is of heroic masculine proportions. Do not be deterred by this imposing beginning, for the rooms that follow are a mix of the splendid and the domestic. Regency furniture, coronation chairs and Chippendale pieces give way to comfortable sofas; Lascelles and Canning portraits by Reynolds and Gainsborough mingle with modern family photos. There are treasures to be seen everywhere: superb Sèvres pieces in the China Room, including a tea service given to Marie Antoinette in 1779, and delightful views of Harewood House by Turner, Girtin and Richmond. The gallery holds Chinese porcelain and Italian pictures including a Tintoretto and a Titian.

Left: Harewood House is an awe-inspiring sight.
Right: The Yellow Drawing Room

HOGHTON TOWER Lancashire

4½ miles (7km) south west of Preston | Open selected days July to September | Tel: 01254 852986 | www.hoghtontower.co.uk

Castellated Hoghton Tower is a prominent landmark for miles around, and at first sight it could almost be a fortified town. The de Hoghton family have owned land here since the Norman Conquest, though the family name is actually Saxon and means 'high wooded hill'. It was Thomas Hoghton who, in 1568, built Hoghton Tower on a hilltop between Preston and Blackburn. He eschewed the prevailing taste for Italian architecture to create a battlemented house that, even at that time, was something of an anachronism. The house has been in the family's unbroken possession ever since. It

was one of the first houses to be opened to the public in 1946.

The founder would surely approve of Hoghton Tower as it is today. Behind the imposing facade the buildings are grouped around two courtyards: one part was for the servants, the other consisting of the banqueting hall and residential rooms.

There are many reminders of a famous visit by King James I, including the King's Bedchamber. Downstairs, in the King's Hall, he laid his hands on two men suffering from scrofula, an ailment held to be curable by a royal touch. In the imposing banqueting hall,

with its minstrel's gallery, the King famously 'knighted' a haunch of beef during one of the many gargantuan feasts this room has witnessed. Another notable visitor was William Shakespeare, who performed in this room with Thomas Hoghton's own troupe of players. Leading off from the banqueting hall is the Ladies' Withdrawing Room, to which the ladies would retire after dinner, leaving the men to pass the port bottle at ever-decreasing intervals.

The banqueting hall, where a haunch of beef was once famously given a knighthood

This handsome neo-Elizabethan mansion and its gardens are located near Morecambe Bay

Holker is the sort of house where, at every turn, you expect to see the hearty clergymen and eager young noblemen, discreet, elderly housemaids and animated younger daughters of the aristocracy straight from the pages of Anthony Trollope. For the Holker that the visitor sees is largely a creation of the third quarter of the 19th century. This former home of the Dukes of Devonshire, preferred by some of them to the splendours of Chatsworth, and still lived in by a branch of the Cavendish family, has its origins in a house built in the 19th century by George Preston, whose family bought land once owned by Cartmel Priory. The estate descended by marriage to the Lowthers, who added the north wing and reconstructed the rest before it eventually came into Cavendish ownership.

The whole house was extensively altered in 1840 by Lord George Cavendish, created Lord Burlington at William IV's coronation.

167

He had it rendered with Roman cement and made romantically Gothic. A disastrous fire in 1871 destroyed the whole of the west wing, including paintings and furniture. The 7th Duke of Devonshire commissioned local architects Paley and Austin – then among the best country-house designers in Britain – to rebuild the wing in pale red sandstone in a grand yet relaxed Elizabethan style, complete with large bay windows and copper dome.

What is notable about a visit to Holker is the lack of restriction: visitors may wander at will through a series of fine, panelled rooms without roping and regimentation. The library sets the tone, with deep armchairs, French furniture and family portraits. Henry

Cavendish, scientist (he discovered nitric acid) and recluse, is remembered by his microscope and copies of his learned works, and there is a portrait by Richmond of Lord Frederick, who was assassinated in Phoenix Park, Dublin, in 1882.

The drawing room retains its original red silk walls, while the spectacular chimneypiece in the dining room, of local marble and finely carved wood – one of several throughout the house – incorporates a Van Dyck self-portrait. Fine craftsmanship is everywhere (every one of the hundred or so balusters of the main staircase is different, for example) and each room retains some of that joyous sense of jewelled clutter loved

The Library contains 3,500 books. Many survived the fire of 1871 and others were brought from Chatsworth

by the Victorians. One of the bedrooms has Wedgwood plaques and blue Jasper Ware on the fire surround; another has furnishings from 1937, when Queen Mary stayed at Holker. The family used to play carpet bowls down the gallery, a spacious and sunny contrast to the hall, which speaks of winter evenings round a roaring fire. In the extensive gardens, formal and informal by turns, is the only surviving monkey puzzle tree planted from seeds that were brought to England in 1837, as well as a superb display of magnolias and rhododendrons.

HUTTON-IN-THE-FOREST Cumbria

7 miles (11km) north west of Penrith | Opening times variable: please check before visiting | Tel: 01768 484449 | **www.hutton-in-the-forest.co.uk**

Sir Gawain is said to have stayed with the Green Knight at Hutton, which was then surrounded by dense woodland. In 1292 Edward I was a visitor during the heyday of the royal hunting forest of Inglewood. However, by the 1350s the de Hoton family found it necessary to build the fortified pele tower as protection against the Scots and the border reivers. The Fletchers bought the property in 1605 and began developing it into a comfortable home. The Long Gallery, rare in the north, was built in 1630, and the classical east front, an unexpected and dramatic addition to this solid house, in the 1680s.

One of the Fletchers was killed fighting for Charles I in 1645. His granddaughter married into the Vane family. The 18th-century Fletcher Vanes improved the garden and grounds rather than the house, and spent much time following country pursuits: one of them employed John Peel, whose portrait hangs in the house, as his huntsman.

Hutton gained its present form in the 1820s, when Salvin designed the dominant south-east tower, and added battlements to the pele. The impressive Stone Hall at its base contrasts with the later rooms, warm with wood panelling, good furniture and family pictures. The charming Cupid Staircase, with its carved cherubs, and the Cupid Room, with its delicate plaster ceiling of 1744, testify to the romantic associations of the house. There is a more formal air about Salvin's dining room, and the Long Gallery retains its Jacobean flavour.

Before you go, take a stroll around the beautiful gardens, which include a delightful walled garden, a woodland walk, terraces, topiary, and three ponds with cascades.

Once surrounded by dense woodland, Hutton now has lovely walled gardens and topiary

KIPLIN HALL North Yorkshire

🐓 **7 miles (11km) east of Richmond** | **Open selected afternoons Easter to end of September** | **Tel: 01748 818178** | **www.kiplinhall.co.uk**

The builder of Kiplin Hall was a local man, George Calvert, who rose from comparatively humble beginnings to the highest political eminence. After graduating from Trinity College, Oxford, he became an MP in 1619. James I made him Secretary of State. In 1625, however, he converted to Roman Catholicism and, as a result, was obliged to resign his post. As compensation, he was given an Irish baronetcy, becoming the 1st Lord Baltimore.

The title was to be significant, for Calvert was to become deeply involved in American affairs. In 1622 James I had granted him Newfoundland, but the climate was not to his liking. Charles I proved more receptive to his complaints and in 1632 he was granted the territories that now comprise Maryland. Unfortunately, he died before the Charter could be issued, so it was his son, Cecilius, who officially founded the state. Both his younger son, Leonard, and his grandson, Charles, were governors of Maryland province, and the city of Baltimore took its name from the family title. Even today, the family maintains its connections with the United States and, though Kiplin Hall is now in the hands of a charitable trust, it has never been sold outside the family.

Kiplin Hall was built in 1622–25. The pretty, three-storey house, built of red brick, is quite delightful. Rectangular in shape, with a square tower in the middle of each side, its rooftops are a forest of chimneys, gables and domes. The widow of the 4th Lord Baltimore married Christopher Crowe, who had been British Ambassador to Leghorn in Italy. He was responsible for carrying out a series of improvements to the house in about 1720, including, most dramatically, replacing the staircases in the north and south towers with a central one.

Seen across the lake from the west, Kiplin Hall's charming rooms include the cosy library, left

3 miles (5km) north of Carnforth | Open selected afternoons May to September | Tel: 01524 734474 | **www.leightonhall.co.uk**

Many of Britain's great houses are situated within acres of beautiful parkland, but few can boast a lovelier setting than Leighton Hall. Behind the house, and beyond the estuary of the River Kent, the mountains of Lakeland create a distinctive backdrop. The theatrical effect is heightened by the Hall's Gothic facade in white limestone.

Leighton Hall's story can be traced as far back as 1246, when Adam d'Avranches built a fortified manor on this site. Every subsequent owner but one has been Roman Catholic, and during Penal Times a priest was always kept hidden in the house. The one exception, George Middleton, was a Civil War cavalier who was both knighted and made baronet on the same day in 1642. Albert Hodgson was the unfortunate incumbent when, during the 1715 Rising, the hall was sacked and burned by Government troops.

It was George Towneley who rebuilt the house, in 1763. He conformed to the tastes of the time by choosing the Adam style. He also laid out the park and gardens. A few years later, in 1800, the Hall underwent a major face-lift, with a castellated facade in the prevailing neo-Gothic style being added to the building. George Towneley died childless, however, and the Hall came into the possession of the Gillow family whose furniture business, based in Lancaster, became famous as a byword for quality.

When Richard Thomas Gillow (known throughout the county as the 'Old Squire') reached the age of seventy, he assumed his days were numbered, and so neglected to carry out more than minor repairs to the fabric of the Hall. In fact he was to live for a further twenty-nine years; as a consequence it was a rather dilapidated Hall that was handed down to his grandson.

There are no roped off areas at Leighton Hall. It retains the atmosphere of a grand but friendly family home

The hallway is a fine example of the Gothic Revival, and through the charming little library is the panelled dining room. The large window in the drawing room offers a panoramic view of the Lakeland mountains – a beautiful outlook from a room full of beautiful examples of Gillow furniture, including a games tables and an ornate lady's work-box. Once the billiards room had been converted into a music room, the house rang to many a musical evening, including a particularly memorable concert by the singer Kathleen Ferrier. The grounds of Leighton Hall should not be missed.

LEVENS HALL Cumbria

🐓 **5 miles (8km) south of Kendal** | **Open selected afternoons April to October** | **Tel: 01539 560321** | **www.levenshall.co.uk**

Levens is pre-eminently an Elizabethan house. Even without the Queen's coat of arms in painted and gilded plasterwork, displayed so prominently above the fireplace in the Great Hall, the building's origins are apparent from the comfortable gables and mullioned windows in the grey rough cast of the exterior. Yet, like many northern houses, it has at its core a defensive pele tower, built by the de Redman family, who held the manor from the 12th century, as protection against Scots invaders. There is also a later 17th-century servants' wing, but it is the grand ground-floor rooms, adapted or added by James Bellingham from around 1580, that are the real pride of Levens.

A century later Bellingham's great-grandson had gambled away the whole estate: it is said that Levens came to Colonel James Grahme, a relative, on the turn of the ace of hearts. It passed, often through the female line, to Grahme's descendants, the Bagots, who still live at Levens. This long, unbroken tradition has created an atmosphere of care and comfort and has ensured that Levens is still full of family furniture and possessions. There are notable plaster ceilings in the main rooms and, in the two drawing rooms, huge carved overmantels, dated 1595. The one in the larger room is heraldic, while the other depicts Hercules and Samson, the elements, the four seasons and the five senses – a typical Elizabethan mixture.

The house has some fine furniture, much of it brought to the house by Colonel Grahme at the end of the 17th century. Grahme, who was Privy Purse and Keeper of the Buckhounds to James II, and his wife Dorothy appear in superb Lely portraits, while

other paintings include a portrait of Anne of Hungary by Rubens. One of the Bagot ancestors married the Duke of Wellington's niece, bringing into the family a number of Napoleonic relics, including his cloak clasp of two bees, taken after Waterloo, and a superb Sèvres chocolate service made for the Emperor's mother. The earliest English patchwork quilt, made by Colonel Grahme's daughters from rare Indian cottons in about 1708, can be found in a dressing room upstairs. The family even owns one of the bowls Sir Francis Drake was using on Plymouth Hoe as the Armada was sighted. The dining room contains the finest set of Charles II walnut chairs in existence. At Levens, there is a superbly achieved balance between relaxed living and show, which makes this house one of the most covetable in the country.

Levens incorporates a Grade I listed garden dating from 1694 – apart from the famous topiary there is a bowling green, a rose garden and herbaceous borders

MEOLS HALL Lancashire

1 mile (1.5km) north of Southport | Open selected afternoons August and September for guided tours | Tel: 01704 228326 | www.meolshall.co.uk

Even when judged by the fluctuating fortunes of many of our country houses, Meols Hall has a chequered history. The Fleetwood and Hesketh families have a long and distinguished pedigree in this part of Lancashire, acquiring both land and upward mobility into the local gentry. Meols Hall came by marriage into the possession of Sir Thomas Hesketh, though unlike the other houses owned by the family, it served merely as a rectory.

Ironically, it took a family disaster to give the Hall a new lease of life. During the 1830s Sir Peter Hesketh-Fleetwood had founded a new town on the Lancashire coast to the north of Blackpool which, without a hint of false modesty, he named Fleetwood. Despite every good intention on his part, this ambitious enterprise foundered. The family estates were sold to settle mounting debts, leaving just Meols Hall to be the family home.

The core of this comfortable house is actually a farmhouse dating back to the 16th and 17th centuries (an engraved stone on a back gable announces a date of 1695). However, in spite of the stylistic clues, the main reconstruction did not take place in the 1720s, as might be supposed, but in the 1960s. The present owner, Roger Fleetwood Hesketh, and his brother Peter, share an avid interest in Georgian architecture, and through their joint endeavours they have incorporated the Hall's two fairly unprepossessing 17th-century wings into their modifications, reviving the Georgian style in a most handsome manner.

The inspiration came from them, while many of the materials – stonework, slates and bricks – were salvaged from other old houses that were being demolished. These recent additions have blended remarkably successfully with the older sections.

Meols Hall is set in one hundred acres of private parkland in the heart of Lancashire

MIREHOUSE Cumbria

Apparently isolated between the severe heights of Skiddaw and the glittering waters of Bassenthwaite Lake, Mirehouse was first built for the 8th Earl of Derby in 1666, sold by him to the Greggs twenty-two years later, and was the meeting place of some of the greatest literary figures of the 19th century. Left in 1802 by the last of the Greggs to John Spedding of nearby Armathwaite Hall, who had sat at the same school desk with Wordsworth, Mirehouse was extended to its present size between 1792 and 1883. What we see today is a traditional family home, full of fine furniture and family pictures. John's son, James, devoted his life to the study of Sir Francis Bacon (some of his collection of Bacon's papers, as well the many volumes Spedding produced about him, are in the Smoking Room) and was an intimate friend of Tennyson, Thackeray and Edward Fitzgerald. It was while staying at Mirehouse that Tennyson, whom Spedding met at Cambridge, walked the shores of Bassenthwaite, composing *Morte d'Arthur*, and the local scenery got into the poem.

Fitzgerald, who was a schoolfriend of Spedding, met Tennyson at Mirehouse, and his chess set can still be seen in the study. Here, too are manuscripts from Wordsworth, Southey and Hartley Coleridge, who were

The bee garden at Mirehouse. The house was the Lake District meeting place of many literary figures

both neighbours and friends of the family. In the library, its bookshelves arranged by the present John Spedding according to Bacon's 'studies', it is his elder brother, Tom, whose portrait has pride of place. A leading Cumberland figure, he too had his literary friends, including Thomas Carlyle, who often called on 'the Genius of the hills' on his way to Scotland. Another Spedding, Anthony, was a friend of John Constable, whose painting of Anthony's Hampstead home hangs in the red-walled Music Room.

175

MUNCASTER CASTLE Cumbria

The Romans built a fort on the edge of the Lake District to protect Ravenglass harbour and the entry to Eskdale. In the Middle Ages, a castle was built on the original Roman foundations. The pele tower still survives beneath later stonework, but virtually everything we see today dates from the 1860s. Lord Muncaster, a member of the Pennington family, who came to Muncaster in 1208, commissioned Salvin to extend and remodel both the medieval remains and a modest 18th-century house, built to his own design by a predecessor. Its situation is wonderful, with a spectacular view over the mountains from the half-mile long terrace, and its gardens full of rhododendrons.

The Victorian building is solid and workmanlike. Two massive towers on the garden front add weight and grandeur to the outside, while inside there are individual touches, like the hall with its enclosed staircase, and the octagonal library, with a brass-railed gallery and fine, vaulted ceiling. The rooms have splendid woodwork and panelling, from Britain and the Continent, and carved chimneypieces, including one by Adam, brought from other houses. The furniture includes both an Elizabethan four-

The Bishop's Room at Muncaster Castle is charmingly cluttered and comfortably appointed

poster and a superb set of Charles II walnut settees and chairs. The house also contains a collection of glittering silverware by Storr and a wonderful series of family portraits from the 17th century to the present.

King Henry VI fled to Muncaster after the Lancastrian defeat at the bloody Battle of Towton in 1461, when 30,000 men died one snowy Sunday. He was found wandering on the fells by a shepherd – the place is now marked by an 18th-century folly tower.

NEWBY HALL Yorkshire

3 miles (5km) south east of Ripon | Open selected afternoons April to September | Tel: 01423 322583 | **www.newbyhall.com**

The present owner of this delightful William and Mary House is descended from William Weddell, who bought it in 1748 with a legacy from his uncle. A man of cultivated tastes, Weddell was a prominent member of the Dilettanti Club and made the Grand Tour of Europe in 1765–66. Returning with a large collection of classical sculptures, he had to enlarge the house to accommodate them all. John Carr of York added the two east wings, remodelled the main block and planned the Statue Gallery, which was completed by Robert Adam.

The red-brick exterior of the Hall, with its stone facings and balustrading, is gracious, but the interiors are the true glory. The beautifully proportioned entrance hall, with its splendid plasterwork, is a suitable introduction to the house. Elegant family portraits by Sir Thomas Lawrence, Pompeo Batoni (the leading painter of English visitors to Rome) and Angelica Kauffman complement the Adam, Chippendale and Hepplewhite furniture. But this is no ordinary house, and there are surprises everywhere. The Circular Room is a delightful William Blackwood design, with ceiling roundels copied from murals at Herculaneum and trompe l'oeil curved doors, painted with classical motifs to look like wall panels. The Motto Bedroom is a charming conceit by Lady Mary Vyner, with old French mottoes painted round the ceiling and on the furniture – even the hip bath has not escaped its worthy proverb.

Two of the rooms are particularly outstanding. The Tapestry Room, completed in 1776, was purpose built to house the glorious Gobelin tapestries ordered from the Paris factory by William Weddell nine years earlier. Woven by Neilson, on a unique dove-grey background, they incorporate medallions of the 'Loves of the Gods' and floral ornaments. Chairs and sofas, specially commissioned by Adam from Chippendale, incorporate matching tapestry upholstery, each depicting a different spray of flowers. This is the only set of Chippendale furniture to retain its original upholstery, and the Gobelin tapestries are one of only five sets made for English patrons. The room has survived quite remarkably in its entirety.

Adam's Statue Gallery is extraordinary for different reasons. Designed in the style of a Roman interior, with two square rooms and a central rotunda, its remarkable plasterwork, alcoves, arches and pedestals provide the perfect setting for Weddell's famous collection of ancient statuary.

Red-brick Newby Hall is attractive from the outside but the interiors are its true glory

PEOVER HALL Cheshire

3 miles (5km) south of Knutsford | Open Monday and Thursday afternoons May to August (except Bank Holidays) | Tel: 01565 632358 | **www.hha.org.uk**

Peover Hall is a mixture of architectural styles. Its pleasant grounds are filled with topiary

The original building that was Peover Hall was replaced in 1585, as an engraved stone over the original entrance reveals, and the house provides a potted history of architectural styles down the years. Peover (pronounced 'Peever') was the brainchild of Sir Randle Mainwaring, whose family had already held land here for centuries.

The irregular exterior of the three-storey house reveals a curious mixture of Tudor and Elizabethan styles; numerous alterations down the years have failed to produce the symmetrical facade no doubt envisaged by Sir Henry Mainwaring, who added a wing about 1760. We can only surmise that his plans extended to demolishing the rest of the old house, and completing the building, but if that was the case, the plan was never carried through. Today some frontages are square, while others are gabled.

Peover Hall is now owned by Randle Brooks, whose good stewardship has extended to a sympathetic remodelling of the house and creating some delightful gardens and wooded parkland. The old Georgian wing, found to be in poor condition, was demolished and replaced by a new block in an Elizabethan style. Peover was requisitioned during World War II by General George Patton of the US Army, and served as his headquarters. Tank tracks can still be identified in the park.

The interior decor, too, reflects personal taste rather than a single unified style. What was once the kitchen is now the Great Hall, dignified by two monumental fireplaces, displays of armour and an unusual ceiling plan in which the beams are laid diagonally. The Long Gallery at the top of the house is open to the pleasing curves of the original Tudor roof timbers; here are displayed many of the family's treasures. The bedrooms are noted for a collection of four-poster beds, pride of place going to an enormous bed, dated 1559, that came from Tamworth Castle.

Peover also has unique Caroline stables, built in 1664, with thirteen wooden stalls and an ornamental plaster ceiling.

178

PRESTON TOWER Northumberland

1 mile (1.5km) south of Chathill | Open daily throughout the year | Tel: 01665 589227 | www.prestontower.co.uk

Some of the north's greatest houses had their origins in defensive pele towers to which, over the centuries, more comfortable quarters have been added. Preston Tower, one of seventy-eight peles listed in 1415, is different. For more than three centuries it barely developed from its original form – and the Preston Tower that we see today is only half of that.

It was built in the 1390s by Sir Robert Harbottle, a trusted friend of Henry IV, who appointed him Sheriff of Northumberland and Constable of Dunstanburgh Castle. Robert was a contemporary of the fiery Harry Hotspur and fought alongside him against the Scots in the Battle of Otterburn in 1388. A display in the Tower illustrates life during those turbulent times. One of Robert's descendants was the gloriously named Sir Guiscard Harbottle, one of six knights killed at Flodden Field in 1513, in hand-to-hand combat with King James IV himself. The Flodden Room in Preston Tower recounts the story of Guiscard's part in the battle, and of Flodden's impact on the history and literature of Scotland and the north.

When England and Scotland were united by James I and VI in 1603, Preston Tower was partially demolished. Stone from two of its towers was used to build adjoining cottages and farm buildings, and the Tower gradually decayed for the next 250 years. It was not until 1864 that Henry Baker Cresswell, whose family had bought the Tower in 1861, came to the rescue. He removed the agricultural additions and built up its rear wall to make it weatherproof. He also added the clock, which he made himself. His home was the Georgian house next door, and part of the Tower was made to hold tanks of water for it, pumped from a nearby spring.

Medieval Preston Tower was constructed during the troubled years of the 1390s

RABY CASTLE County Durham

The intensely romantic building we see today was begun in the 14th century. Romance was not, of course, its purpose. When the Nevill family built Raby there were constant threats from Scotland, and the surrounding landscape was harsh and unwelcoming. The 30 foot- (9m-) curtain wall has long since gone, but the huge feudal castle, which grew gradually through the generations, retains much of its medieval impressiveness.

It was here that Richard III's mother, Cicely Nevill, 'The Rose of Raby', was brought up by her father, the 1st Earl of Westmorland.

The royal connection did not help the 6th Earl, who led the Rising of the North in 1569, intended to put Mary, Queen of Scots on the throne. Defeated, he fled abroad and Raby was taken by the Crown. After more than fifty years of neglect, it was sold to the Vane family. The second Sir Henry Vane to live at Raby was executed by Charles II, but the Vanes eventually became Barons Barnard, Earls of Darlington and Dukes of Cleveland. The last Duke died in 1891, and Raby is now owned by Lord Barnard.

Approached through the gatehouse is the awesome bulk of Clifford's Tower, built in about 1378. Other reminders of the original castle are Bulmer's Tower and the perfect 14th-century kitchen, with its ox-sized fireplaces, and the servants' hall. The spectacular Nevill Gateway leads to the cobbled Inner Court. The long tunnel was created by John Carr when he restored and reshaped the castle in the 1760s.

The magnificent contents of the castle were all collected after the 1st Lord Barnard, furious at his son's marriage, sold everything in 1714. Favourite of many visitors is the marble statue of a Greek slave girl by Powers.

14th-century Raby Castle has warlike battlemented towers but a surprisingly cosy medieval kitchen

RIPLEY CASTLE Yorkshire

The colourful and eccentric Ingilbys have lived at Ripley Castle since the 1320s, when Thomas Ingilby married Edeline Thweng, heiress to the estate. Despite attaining high office in the judiciary, he is best remembered for saving the life of Edward III when he was attacked by a wounded boar while hunting. This act of valour won Thomas a knighthood, but the Ingilby's catholicism cost them dear. Sir William joined the conspirators in the 'Pilgrimage of Grace' and was saved from execution by Henry VIII only because he had advised against taking action. His son, Francis, trained as a Jesuit priest in the seminary at Rheims, returning to England in 1584; captured two years later, he was convicted of treason and hung, drawn and quartered at York. Beatified in 1987, he is the only Ingilby likely to become a Saint. His brother, William, narrowly avoided execution for treason when he was unjustly implicated in the Gunpowder Plot.

Loyalty to the Crown proved equally hazardous: Sir William was fined over £700 for 'delinquency' in supporting Charles I during the Civil War, and his son briefly fled into exile with James II. More prosaically, in 1794, the then baronet and his wife abandoned their six small children when escaping to Europe to avoid their creditors. It was ten years before he could pay off their debts and return home.

The medieval fortifications of Ripley Castle were built to provide protection from marauding Scots, but later baronets added a 16th-century tower and an 18th-century mansion house. Designed by John Carr of York, this is the most elegant part of the castle, with furniture by Chippendale (whose father was a joiner on the Ripley estate) and Hepplewhite. The Continental residence of various Ingilbys, both enforced and voluntary, is reflected in the Venetian chandeliers and Italian plasterwork ceilings and statuary.

Most fascinating of all are the tower rooms: the library, with its huge 18th-century table, 5,000 books and the 1386 foundation charter of Mount Grace Priory; above it, the Tower Room, with a fabulous plasterwork ceiling, where James I slept in 1603 and, on the third storey, the gem of the castle, the perfectly preserved Knight's Chamber of 1555. Interesting features include a priest hole hidden behind the panelling and the door leading to a spiral staircase that has a prominent false handle to delay attackers.

Romantic Ripley Castle has a waterfall in its grounds

RODE HALL Cheshire

The Wilbrahams have been a notable Cheshire family since the 13th century, and before the present Hall was built, a timber-framed house occupied this site. Then, in about 1700, Randle Wilbraham built a house of such modest proportions that within a few years it had been downgraded to become the servants' quarters. It wasn't until the present Hall was built, in the middle of the 18th century, that the Wilbrahams finally occupied a family seat that properly reflected their position in society. The architect is thought to have been John Hope, best known for designing the Piece Hall in Halifax.

It was Randle Wilbraham III who had the house refaced in stucco during yet another extensive programme of renovation in the early part of the 19th century. This redundant stucco was, however, removed in 1927, and it is once again a handsome red-brick house that greets visitors at the end of the driveway, albeit a house that reflects a distinctly convoluted architectural history.

Many of the rooms retain their Regency elegance, including the delightful library with its original fitted bookcases designed by Gillow. The main staircase, still blessed with carved balusters and rococo plasterwork, is now the only room in the house to have kept its Georgian features.

The oval ante-room has been redecorated in Regency style, with walls of the deepest blue to set off a collection of gouache paintings. The dining room betrays the handiwork of architect Lewis Wyatt: cool, elegant and almost entirely unadorned. Above the black marble fireplace is a portrait of Randle Wilbraham, the owner responsible for the building of the house in the 1750s.

Rode Hall's present Grecian-style portico was probably added in about 1820

ROKEBY PARK County Durham

If buildings could fly like homing pigeons, Rokeby Park would surely wing its way from its northern perch to the Venetian mainland. For this ochre-painted house is a villa in the purest Palladian style; a poised composition of a tall central block and lower, retiring wings, all with pyramid roofs, following in its wake. The house was designed by Sir Thomas Robinson, for himself, on the site of the old Robinson mansion – some distance from the still-surviving medieval tower of the Rokeby family, from whom the Robinsons bought the estate during the Civil War. 'Long Sir Tom' was the son-in-law of the Earl of Carlisle, for whom Vanbrugh was building the baroque Castle Howard, but Robinson's taste was for the neoclassical style. Rokeby was to be both a home and a show place.

The lower ground-floor rooms are not lofty, but each has its characteristic decoration, especially the breakfast room, enlivened with cut-out 18th-century prints. But it was on the *piano nobile* – the main floor – that Robinson expended most of his talent and money. The music room is a fitting introduction to the grandeur of Rokeby's principal room. The full height of the house, the Saloon should be filled with the music of Handel for full effect, for it is of the same stately richness, from its gilded ceiling to the marble fireplaces and the doorways, surrounded by columns and crowned with triangular pediments.

Palladian Rokeby House was the setting for Sir Walter Scott's ballad 'Rokeby'

An MP, Sir Tom was nearly always in debt because of his high living, and spent a period of time as Governor of Barbados to escape his creditors. When in London he was a director of entertainments at Ranelagh Gardens, and he appears both in Hogarth's picture *The Beggar's Opera* and in Fielding's novel *Joseph Andrews*. He sold Rokeby to John Sawrey Morritt, whose family still lives here. It was Morritt's son who acquired the Velasquez painting known as *The Rokeby Venus*, which hung in the Saloon until it went to the National Gallery.

183

RYDAL MOUNT Cumbria

1½ miles (2.5km) north of Ambleside | Open selected days throughout the year | Tel: 015394 33002 | **www.rydalmount.co.uk**

Rydal Mount owes its fame to its most famous tenant, William Wordsworth. He came to this lime-washed yeoman's house on May Day 1813. 'The weather is delightful and the place a Paradise,' wrote his sister Dorothy, and it was to remain his home until his death in 1850. His was a large household – it included not only the poet and his wife Mary, but his three surviving children and Mary's sister Sarah Hutchinson, as well as Dorothy. The move was partly financed by Wordsworth's appointment as Distributor of Stamps for Westmorland, which brought him his first (and only) steady income, and earned Browning's scorn: 'Just for a handful of silver he left us,' he wrote in *The Lost Leader,* 'Just for a riband to stick in his coat.'

More than half of Wordsworth's published poetry was written at Rydal Mount, a house with origins in a farm built in 1550: the dining room still has its early timbers and slate floor and was enlarged about the middle of the 18th century. Wordsworth was particularly attracted to the traditional style of the house, as well as by its spectacular views over Rydal Water and Windermere. He never owned the house (leased from the le Flemings of nearby Rydal Hall) and so did little to alter

Tucked away in lush gardens, Rydal Mount was a place of peace and inspiration for William Wordsworth

it. Wordsworth believed that a house and its garden should harmonize with each other and with the locality. The garden, one of the most important of its date, is still much as he left it, with terraces stretching across the hillside. The highest was already there when he took over the house, but he added two others, one so that Dorothy could be pushed in her invalid chair to enjoy the view. Wordsworth would pace along behind them, booming new poems to himself.

SEATON DELAVAL HALL Northumberland

By the time Sir John Vanbrugh came to design his masterpiece at Seaton Delaval he had already produced both Castle Howard and Blenheim Palace. Never one for tame classical copying, he used the opportunity given by Admiral George Delaval to build a house on this windswept northern coast to indulge his taste for the dramatic – and dramatic Seaton Delaval certainly is. As a former playwright, Vanbrugh knew how to utilize scenery for impressive effect, and the north-facing entrance front of his main block – strangely, it largely ignores the sea – is hugely powerful, almost aggressive, with its towers and turrets and the enormous columns casting sinister shadows that dwarf the central doorway. Even the garden front is monumentally and magnificently intimidating.

From the outside, the Hall looks whole and complete, but the Great Hall of the central block is semi-ruinous, open to the roof and still bearing the marks of the fire that swept through it. Blackened statues stand in their niches and a delicate iron gallery, now restored, gives access to vanished floors. In the Mahogany and Tapestry Rooms on the north side there is a display of family portraits and documents, and some rare mahogany panelling survives, while the vaulted basement could have held supplies for an army. In the west wing, open only by special appointment, the former kitchen is now the entrance hall, and in this and the other habitable rooms are furniture and paintings that were rescued from the blaze, as well as items from Melton Constable in Norfolk. Over in the opposite wing, Vanbrugh's fine stables, like a pagan temple, still have the horses' names above the classical niches holding their mangers. The stalls have their original finely moulded timberwork and paved floors.

Fireplace inside the central block, where the principal rooms were housed before being gutted by fire in 1822

There is a great 14th-century tower at the heart of Sizergh Castle, the original part of a building that had the misfortune to be within a wide band of the country that, at that time, frequently changed hands between England and Scotland. This pele tower is still recognizable, but a great deal of building was carried out during Tudor times, extending the castle to the north and west and adding a great chamber over the old hall.

Most of the interior now reflects this time of prosperity and expansion, with superb oak panelling and some outstanding carving.

The intricate panelling of the Inlaid Chamber was sold in 1891 to the Victoria and Albert Museum, but they have kindly loaned two panels back to Sizergh so that visitors can imagine how the room would have looked in its heyday. The museum have also loaned the inlaid bed, which had been made to match the room.

In 1239 Sizergh Castle was brought into the Strickland family by its heiress, and their descendant still lives here today, although the family gave the castle to the National Trust in 1950. Their occupancy of the castle was unbroken throughout that period except for a short time when the family accompanied James II into exile. Their support of the Stuart cause is reflected in many of the portraits on display in the house.

Sir Thomas Strickland was given the honour of carrying the banner of St George – England's premier banner – to the Battle of Agincourt in 1415.

The north west front (below) and the drawing room (right) at Sizergh Castle

SLEDMERE HOUSE Yorkshire

Descended from successful Yorkshire merchants, the family of Sir Tatton Sykes can trace their ownership of Sledmere House back in an unbroken line to the middle of the 17th century. It was Richard Sykes, a High Sheriff of Yorkshire, who demolished the old Tudor house and began construction of a new red-brick mansion in 1751. His brother, 'Parson Sykes', created a baronet for his pioneering agricultural work, inherited the estate and it was his son, Sir Christopher, who transformed the house. Acting as his own architect, though consulting John Carr and Samuel Wyatt, he encased the house in Nottinghamshire stone and added new ranges to the north and south. He then

Beautiful landscaped gardens (above) and the amazing Turkish room with its inlaid Syrian table (left)

engaged 'Capability' Brown to landscape his 2,000 acres (809ha) of parkland – a job that entailed demolishing the old village and rebuilding it out of sight to the east.

A disastrous fire in 1911 left only the four walls standing, though an efficient salvage operation saved virtually all the contents of the house. It was rebuilt, to the original designs, by the York architect, Walter Brierley, who reinstated plasterwork from the original moulds and redecorated the house following contemporary watercolours of the rooms.

The grim and forbidding aspect of the exterior is entirely belied by the opulence of the interior. Remarkably intricate plasterwork ceilings and friezes, picked out in paint and gold, are a feature of every room: each one is different, though classical themes prevail – note the lyre motif in the music room, which houses the famous Sledmere organ created for the original house. Pillars of every order, classical statuary and plaster reliefs are an ever-present reminder of the 18th-century obsession with the antique.

STOCKELD PARK Yorkshire

The Middleton family originally lived in this delightful country house. Wealthy landed gentry, owning extensive estates in the rich agricultural lands between York, Harrogate and Ripon, they commissioned a Palladian-style mansion from James Paine, the celebrated architect, who, at only nineteen, was responsible for supervising the construction of Nostell Priory, near Wakefield. Stockeld Park, built between 1758 and 1763, is one of the finest examples of his work.

The agricultural depression at the end of the 19th century forced the Middletons to put the estate up for auction. Like many other Yorkshire country houses, it was bought by a successful textile magnate, Robert Foster.

He was the grandson of the founder of Black Dyke Mills at Queensbury.

Robert Foster might not have had the ancestry of the Middletons, but he certainly had the finances that they lacked. He built a substantial new wing onto the house for his domestic staff, turned the old chapel into a library and converted the orangery into a new chapel in the grounds. He even altered the approach to the house, closing the old drive from the south lodge and building a new one from the north. This required major engineering works, raising the level of the new drive and building a new portico.

The house is approached through parkland and the main entrance leads straight into the charming Oval Hall. An elegant cantilevered circular staircase, with crinoline balustrading, defies gravity to soar several storeys; even the doors off the hall are curved to match its oval contours. Large windows make the house light and airy and give wonderful views of the surrounding parkland and woods. In the library is a fireplace that belonged to the Queen Mother. Furniture and pictures collected by several generations of Fosters add a personal touch to this pleasant house, which is anything but a museum showpiece.

Stockeld Park is primarily an agricultural estate and is known as Yorkshire's finest Christmas tree grower

WALLINGTON Northumberland

🐓 **10 miles (16km) west of Morpeth** | **Open selected days March to end of October** | **Tel: 01670 773967** | **www.nationaltrust.org.uk**

At the heart of a great moorland estate, this square William and Mary mansion has a surprise for visitors. In the midst of all its splendour and its exceptionally beautiful plasterwork, its exquisite collections of porcelain and its fine works of art, Wallington's central hall is a curiosity. It is a grand, galleried hall made cosy; a lofty formal area altered to be lived in. The pillars and arches are painted with plants and flowers, undertaken by Lady Trevelyan and her friends (including John Ruskin), and the main panels are painted with dramatic scenes from Northumbrian history by William Bell Scott. Sir William and Lady Trevelyan were renowned for their eccentricity and charm, and this room is a fitting illustration of their occupancy of Wallington.

Elsewhere in the house visitors will be charmed again, by the collection of dolls' houses and model soldiers, by the kitchen, filled with Victorian utensils and appliances, and by Lady Wilson's Cabinet of Curiosities. This diverse collection includes antiquities, stuffed birds, narwhal tusks, documents relating to Wallington and a model of a Jerusalem church. The house is set in 100 acres (40ha) of lawns, lakes and woodland, with a lovely walled garden and a conservatory housing tender plants.

Below: The curved gravel drive leading to the east front of Wallington

Right: The magnificent Central Hall, designed by John Dobson of Newcastle and built in 1853–54

1	**Abbotsford** Melrose	194
2	**Arniston House** Midlothian	195
3	**Ayton Castle** Border	196
4	**Ballindalloch Castle** Moray	198
5	**Blair Castle** Perth & Kinross	199
6	**Bowhill** Border	200
7	**Braemar Castle** Aberdeenshire	201
8	**Cawdor Castle** Highland	202
9	**Dalmeny House** City of Edinburgh	203
10	**Drumlanrig Castle** D & G	204
11	**Duart Castle** Isle of Mull	205
12	**Dunrobin Castle** Highland	206
13	**Dunvegan Castle** Isle of Skye	207
14	**Falkland Palace** Fife	208
15	**Floors Castle** Border	209
16	**Glamis Castle** Angus	210
17	**Hopetoun House** City of Edinburgh	211
18	**Inveraray Castle** Argyll & Bute	212
19	**Manderston** Border	214
20	**Mellerstain House** Border	216
21	**Paxton House** Border	217
22	**Scone Palace** Perth & Kinross	218
23	**Thirlestane Castle** Border	219
24	**Traquair House** Border	220

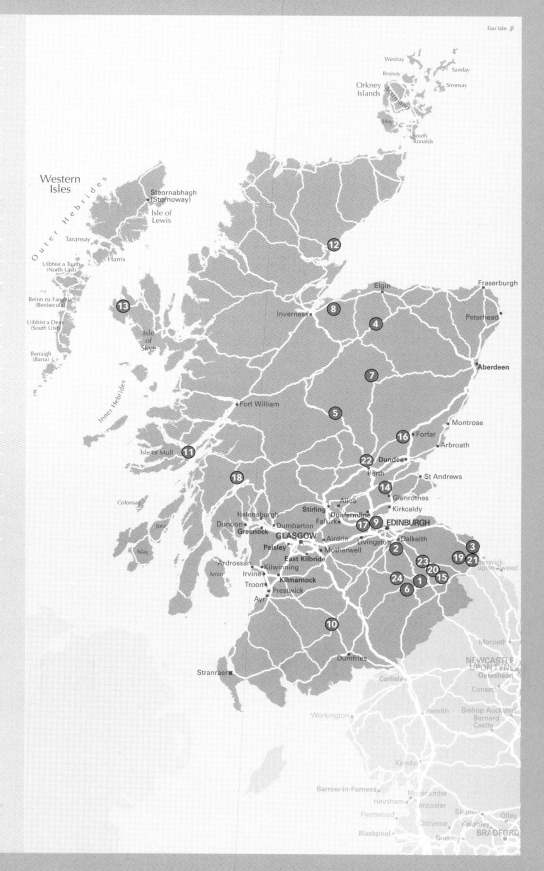

SCOTLAND & THE BORDERS | 5

Scottish novelist and poet Sir Walter Scott (1771–1832) played a major role in creating today's image of romantic Scotland, and his house, Abbotsford, on the Tweed, below the enchanting Eildon Hills, is testimony to his enthusiasms. His family, the Scotts of Buccleuch, own two of the grandest houses in all Scotland – Bowhill and Drumlanrig – both packed with fabulous treasures. Meanwhile, the simple old Border laird's home of Traquair, which has played host to innumerable kings, is perhaps the most romantic house in all Britain. Further north, the grim MacLeod fastness of Dunvegan, on the Isle of Skye, can claim Britain's nastiest dungeon and Glamis its particularly chilling monster, while the country's only remaining private army is based at Blair Castle. But Scottish history is not all violence – far from it – and all the graces of civilization will be found in the 18th-century magnificence of Hopetoun House, the Scots Baronial ducal splendours of Dunrobin and Inveraray, the 19th-century Gothic of Scone Palace and the Edwardian opulence of Manderston.

ABBOTSFORD Melrose

2 miles (3km) south east of Galashiels | Open selected days March to October | Tel: 01896 752043 | **www.scottsabbotsford.co.uk**

By 1811, at the age of forty, Walter Scott could at last see financial security on the horizon. In 1805 he had established his popularity as a poet with the historical ballad *The Lay of the Last Minstrel* and had followed this to great acclaim with the heroic *Marmion* and the romantic ballad *The Lady of the Lake*. With the prospect of considerable earnings from his future writings, Scott borrowed half the £4,000 needed to purchase the farm of Cartley Hole. The site was indifferent for farming, but Scott could see its potential, and threw his prodigious energies into creating a modest country cottage. Adding an armoury,

a dining room, a study, a conservatory and three bedrooms to the existing farmhouse, he called it Abbotsford, after the river crossing below the house and its situation on land once owned by the abbey at Melrose.

By 1812 the family was ready to move in, and in that first summer, Scott spent every spare moment supervising the planting of the estate with oak and Spanish chestnut, while furiously composing *Rokeby* to pay for it all. In fact, the building of Abbotsford signalled the period of Scott's greatest creativity, for in 1814 he started the series of *Waverley* novels that would establish his lasting fame. In 1822

the remains of the farmhouse at Abbotsford were demolished, making way for the main block, which can be seen today, complete with courtyard walls. Chief architect was William Atkinson, a noted castle-builder, but Scott and his friends added their own ideas.

The house has great character, mixing Tudor and traditional Scottish styles, and its contents powerfully reflect their creator, for it is the treasure-house of a magpie with a gift for romantic history.

Abbotsford is at the heart of a landscape that inspired the literary works of its creator, Sir Walter Scott

ARNISTON HOUSE Midlothian

Arniston House is the family seat of the Dundas family, who first became established in the area in the 12th century, though the first house on this site was built in the early part of the 17th century. In the 18th century Robert Dundas presided over the Court of Session, Scotland's supreme civil law court, and it was he who commissioned Adam to design a Palladian family seat that would be worthy of their status. Robert's son, Henry, ascended to the peerage as 1st Viscount Melville – there is a statue of him in St Andrew Square in Edinburgh.

The house contains a wealth of family portraits, from the 16th century onwards, including works by Ramsay and Raeburn; the faces that look down from the walls contrive to be striking without any trace of aggression – a quality that is by no means universal in Scottish family portraits. John and William Adam's splendid mansion incorporates some of the original house, notably the panelled Oak Room, but fireplaces and decorative features were added. Other rooms, including the drawing room, dining room and library, have notable plasterwork and intricate friezes characteristic of Adam's work, while the kitchen still has its Victorian food lift.

This is a house that has been continuously inhabited by members of the same family. The current owners, the Dundas-Bekkers, have devoted a great deal of time and energy into attacking an outbreak of dry rot and are engaged in an ongoing programme of restoration. This does mean that parts of the house are closed off from time to time, but there remains plenty to see.

Outside, the grounds have developed over the centuries too, from formal layouts to the more natural landscapes in the style of 'Capability' Brown. There is also an orangery.

The south exterior (top) and the library (right) at Arniston House

AYTON CASTLE Border

Though Ayton Castle is a true creation of the Victorian age, there has been a castle on the site since Norman times. In the 15th century it was owned by the Homes, but was confiscated by the Crown because of their support for the Stuart cause. In the mid-18th century, the estate was acquired by James Fordyce, who was the Scottish Commissioner for Lands and Forests. At that time the estate was important and rich enough to instigate the removal of Ayton village to a more distant location. That castle was completely devastated by fire in the early years of the 19th century.

The basis of the Ayton Castle we see today was commissioned by the 19th-century owner, William Mitchell-Innes, who chose Gillespie Graham to create for him a

suitably grand, though not excessively large, residence: he was a practical man, who saw no need for rooms he could not utilize. His son, however, had a much larger family and found it necessary to extend Ayton soon after he inherited it in 1860.

In addition to adding new rooms, including an attic suite of nurseries, the castle was splendidly redecorated and the rich plasterwork of the ceilings remains a particularly fine feature. In 1886 the castle was sold to Henry Liddell, a Northumberland landowner, and it is the widow of his grandson, David Liddell-Grainger, who is the present owner.

Wintry Ayton Castle viewed from the village road (top), the library (right) and the drawing room (far right)

BALLINDALLOCH CASTLE Moray

29 miles (47km) north east of Aviemore | Open April to September | Tel: 01807 500205 | www.ballindallochcastle.co.uk

One of the most beautiful castles in Scotland, Ballindalloch nestles at the heart of the beautiful Spey valley, with the majestic mountains of the Cairngorm Massif rising to the south, and the waters of the rivers Spey and Avon flowing through the grounds. Known, fittingly, as 'the Pearl of the North', Ballindalloch has been home to the Macpherson-Grants since 1546 and is one of the few privately owned castles to have been lived in continuously by the original family.

Built originally in the traditional Z plan, Ballindalloch illustrates the development from the fortified tower house of the 16th century to the elegant Highland country house so admired by the Victorians. The house today is very much a lived-in home, but filled with family memorabilia, an important collection of 17th-century Spanish paintings and some fine furniture.

The Hall, designed by architect Thomas MacKenzie in the 1850s, has an unusual umbrella design and fan vaulting. Of interest in this room are a Sheraton corner cupboard by Ridgeway, c.1820; a fine bureau plat (writing table) of Louis XV period; and a set of Scottish chairs made in Chinese Chippendale style, with unusual carvings of bells. Some 18th-century pistols hang over the fireplace; Scottish dirks on display were used for hunting or dealing with enemies. The dining room – originally the Great Hall of the Castle – was redesigned during the 1850 renovations and panelled in American pine. The magnificent fireplace, with the Macpherson and Grant coats of arms above, was installed at the same time.

In the grounds are a superb rock garden, with tumbling spring water, laid out in 1937 by the 5th Baronet, and a walled garden, redesigned in 1996 to celebrate the Castle's 450th anniversary – a haven of beauty.

Ballindalloch Castle is set in magnificent grounds between the Rivers Spey and Avon

BLAIR CASTLE

14 miles (22km) north west of Pitlochry | Open daily from March to October | Tel: 01796 481207 | **www.blair-castle.co.uk**

The Murrays have lived at Blair Atholl since the earldom was conferred in 1629 on John Murray, Master of Tullibardine, but the history of the castle and the family dates back to David Strathbogie, the Crusader Earl of Atholl.

James Murray inherited the Atholl title on his father's death in 1724, and started on an ambitious scheme to create a new park and drastically 'improve' the castle. It is largely his work that we see inside the building today, as he turned a simple fortified castle into one of the finest Georgian residences in the country.

The 3rd Duke died in 1774, and his son John, the 4th Duke, retained the title for fifty-six peaceful years. His influence at Blair was considerable, and he earned the nickname 'the planting Duke' for his extensive afforestation of the estate.

The 7th Duke inherited in 1864, taking the name Stewart-Murray, and he was largely responsible for turning what had become a Georgian mansion back into a romantic castle in the best Scottish tradition. He engaged the architects David and John Bryce, noted for their specialist skills in the Scots Baronial style. Crow-stepped gables and blue-slate-roofed pepperpot towers were fully restored and Cumming's Tower was rebuilt to its original height. The entrance hall was added along with the magnificent ballroom, which is popular still for Highland balls and grand dinners.

The 8th Duchess was the formidable Katherine Marjorie Ramsay, an accomplished musician, who organized concerts for soldiers in the Boer War and World War I. She opened the castle to the public in 1936, and in the first year a remarkable 32,500 visitors came to admire and enjoy the Atholl home and lands. It remains the most popular private castle visited in Scotland.

Highland cattle graze in fields near the castle and the native red squirrel can often be spotted in the area

BOWHILL Border

3 miles (5km) west of Selkirk | Open daily July and August | Tel: 01750 22204 | **www.bowhill.org**

'Sweet Bowhill' was Sir Walter Scott's fond name for this fine house in his *Lay of the Last Minstrel*, and he spoke with authority: as a kinsman of the owners, he was a frequent visitor. The Scott family had been prominent in Scottish history since the 13th century, amassing vast tracts of land in the Borders, including the Bowhill estate. One Sir Walter Scott fought with James IV at Flodden; another, knighted by James VI, was known as 'Bold Buccleuch' for his daring deeds in Border raids during the 16th century; he was created 1st Lord Scott of Buccleuch.

In 1663 Anna, the heiress to the Scotts, married James, Duke of Monmouth, natural son of Charles II, who was then created Duke of Buccleuch and Earl of Dalkeith (another Scott property). She had been granted the title Duchess of Buccleuch in her own right and so avoided the forfeiture of her position and estates when her husband was executed after his unsuccessful uprising.

A succession of marriages brought further titles and possessions to the Scotts, who are among the oldest families in Scotland, and Bowhill remains their main residence. Amidst beautiful forest and farmland between two tributaries of the Tweed, this imposing mansion contains some magnificent paintings, including works by Van Dyck, Canaletto, Reynolds, Gainsborough and Claude Lorraine, an outstanding collection of portrait miniatures and a fine display of porcelain and furniture. Two rooms in the house are devoted to memorabilia associated with the Duke of Monmouth and Sir Walter Scott.

The Minstrel tea room is worth a visit and has recently received a Healthy Living Award.

The well-proportioned entrance hall of Bowhill House is hung with portraits and dates from the early part of the 19th century

BRAEMAR CASTLE Aberdeenshire

½ mile (0.8km) east of Braemar | Open selected days Easter to end of October | Tel: 01339 741219 | www.braemarcastle.co.uk

Its strategic location on the main route through the mountains has meant a turbulent history for Braemar Castle; not only has it changed hands several times, but it has also been burnt out and deserted, and used as a garrison fort for Hanoverian troops determined to crush any further Highland rebellion. Later fitted out in the best 19th-century traditions of elegance, style and comfort, it is today the delightful family home of the Farquharsons of Invercauld.

The castle was started in 1628 by John Erskine, Earl of Mar, to fend off his belligerent neighbours along the valley – the Farquharsons, the Gordons and the Forbes – and its original structure as an L-shaped tower-house can still be seen. The Earl of Mar was an important figure in Scottish politics, holding the positions of High Treasurer of Scotland and guardian to the young King James VI (later James I of England).

The first serious conflict arose in 1689. While the Earl of Mar supported the Hanoverian government, his neighbours the Farquharsons favoured the doomed Jacobite cause, and rallied to support the stand made by John Graham of Claverhouse ('Bonnie Dundee'). The Hanoverian troops on the trail of Claverhouse, under General Mackay, stopped off at Braemar Castle, but were routed by the Farquharsons in a surprise night-attack. The Farquharson leader, John, 'The Black Colonel', ordered the castle to be burned, to prevent its further use by government troops, and for sixty years it remained a forlorn, burnt-out shell.

Braemar Castle was rebuilt, and remains one of the best examples of a Hanoverian fort. Turrets were extended, a rectangular rampart was constructed with projecting salients to make the classic eight-point star shape, and the interior was worked on by the two young sons of the great architect William Adam, one of whom, Robert, would later outstrip his father's fame.

Braemar Castle, seat of clan Farquharson, was a 17th-century hunting lodge and Hanoverian garrison

CAWDOR CASTLE Highland

5 miles (8km) south west of Nairn | Open daily May to October | Tel: 01667 404401 | **www.cawdorcastle.com**

The early Thanes of Caider (early spelling) were appointed Sheriffs and Constables of Nairn. A thane was a kind of feudal baron holding land from the Crown, and was often a clan chief and a powerful individual answerable only to the King and to God. Not much is known of Donald, the 1st Thane of Cawdor, but his successor, William, 2nd Thane, received a Charter of Thanage from King Robert the Bruce in 1310. This confirmed his hereditary thanedom and began a family line that survives to this day at Cawdor.

The tower fortress of Cawdor Castle remained virtually unchanged until the 17th century when Sir Hugh Campbell, 15th Thane of Cawdor, transformed the simple

tower fortress into an elegant and spacious mansion. A large family of nine children and a generous household of twenty-seven servants dictated the size somewhat, but the changes, both to the building and the interior, are a tribute to Sir Hugh's good taste and sense of style. The massive project was started in 1684 and not finished until 1702. Sir Hugh supervised the whole proceedings, ensuring the craftsmen completed everything in 'the handsomest order, so themselves may have credit and Sir Hugh satisfaction.' The workers were paid partly in silver coins and partly in ground cereals.

After Sir Hugh's death in 1716 the estate was passed to his grandson John, 17th

Cawdor Castle is surrounded by three gardens: the walled garden, the flower garden and the wild garden

Thane of Cawdor, but it was a period of civil unrest, notably the Jacobite Risings, and John decided that it would be prudent to move his family to a safer environment. The family divided their time between London and their estates in Wales, leaving Cawdor in the capable stewardship of John's uncle, Sir Archibald Campbell. As a peace-loving man, Sir Archibald kept well away from the political wranglings of the time and contented himself with creating a new garden at Cawdor and undertaking a programme of improvements, both interior and exterior, of the castle.

DALMENY HOUSE

3 miles (5km) east of South Queensferry, 4 miles (6km) west of Edinburgh | Open some afternoons May to July | Tel: 0131 331 1888 | **www.dalmeny.co.uk**

The original building here, Barnbougle, was a 13th-century castle, built on the seashore by the Mowbray Family. In 1662 Sir Archibald Primrose, father of the 1st Earl of Rosebery, bought the Dalmeny Estate and lived in Barnbougle Castle, but by the end of the 18th century the castle was in a bad state of repair. The Earl refused to make improvements, believing it was good enough for them to live in. His son, the 4th Earl, did not agree, and decided to build another dwelling, which he named Dalmeny House.

In 1814 two architects – William Wilkins and Jeffrey Wyatt – were commissioned to submit plans for the house. The 4th Earl preferred Wyatt's Tudor Gothic design to Wilkins' neo-Classical Greek style, but he obviously felt some loyalty to Wilkins because they had been at Cambridge together. He asked Wilkins to submit another design in the Tudor Gothic style, accepted it, and Dalmeny

House was born. Not only did Wilkins design the house, he also designed some of the furniture, including sofas, stools and chairs. Twenty-nine sets of chimneys, numerous battlements, embrasures and turret shafts, at the then quite substantial cost of almost £5,000, were shipped from London. It is thought that Dalmeny House became the inspiration for many 19th-century Scottish houses, by architects such as William Burn and David Bruce.

The entrance hall has a stunning hammer-beam ceiling and a rare set of tapestries designed by Goya to be hung in Spanish royal palaces: only two sets exist outside Spain, and the Queen has the other. Several family portraits adorn the walls and there are two marble busts by Ernst Boehm, one of Lord Rosebery and the other of Gladstone, who stayed at Dalmeny House during the Midlothian Campaign.

Part of a famous collection of French furniture collected by Baron Mayer Rothschild is in the drawing room, brought into the family by Rothschild's only child, Hannah, who married the 5th Earl. Beauvais tapestries, designed in 1740 by Francois Boucher in Chinoiserie style, depict European fantasies of what life in China might be like. A number of Sèvres pieces are also on display, as well as busts of Louis XVI and Marie Antoinette.

Lord Rosebery's Sitting Room has been kept as it would have looked in the 6th Earl's lifetime. Around the room are paintings of racehorses and a display of the Rosebery rose and primrose racing colours. The link with racing goes back over 100 years when Baron Mayer founded a stud at Mentmore.

The bronze statue of a horse ouside the house reveals Dalmeny's long connection with horseracing

DRUMLANRIG CASTLE Dumfries & Galloway

8 miles (13km) north of Dumfries | Open daily March to end of August | Tel: 01848 331555 | **www.drumlanrig.com**

Drumlanrig was a Douglas stronghold as far back as the 14th century and Sir James Douglas was the right-hand man of Robert Bruce, King of Scotland. Indeed, the family crest of a winged heart surmounted by Bruce's crown, which appears throughout the house, stems from that alliance.

The present palatial structure was built around the original castle by William Douglas, 1st Duke of Queensberry. An impressive horseshoe staircase and colonnaded archway lead up to the castle entrance. Masterpieces such as Leonardo da Vinci's *Madonna with the Yarnwinder*, Hans Holbein the Younger's *Sir Nicholas Carew* and Rembrandt's *Old Woman Reading* adorn the Staircase Hall.

A tour of the castle reveals room after room of priceless works of art, from the exquisite Grinling Gibbons carvings and Meissen porcelain Monkey Band in the drawing room to the Dutch and Flemish paintings in the Boudoir. From the early Douglases to the present-day guardians of the estate, the family motto of 'Forward' has true meaning. Rural land management and woodland conservation, combined with shrewd business sense, ensures that stately Drumlanrig Castle and all its treasures can be enjoyed for generations to come.

Drumlanrig Castle has played host to many celebrity guests throughout its history, from Mary, Queen of Scots to the first moon-walking astronaut, Neil Armstrong. No-one's visit has been more commemorated, however, than that of Prince Charles Edward Stuart (Bonnie Prince Charlie). The bedroom that he occupied on his retreat northwards on 22 December 1745 has been dedicated to his memory. A pastel of the Prince and an oil painting of his father hang either side of one window and several personal items, including his money box, rings, some miniatures and a camp kettle, are on display.

Drumlanrig Castle is a fine example of late 17th-century Renaissance architecture

DUART CASTLE Isle of Mull

3 miles (5km) south east of Craignure ferry port | **Open selected days April to October** | **Tel: 01680 812309** | **www.duartcastle.com**

Duart would not be the fine castle it is today had it not been for the determination and foresight of Sir Fitzroy Maclean, 14th Baronet and great-grandfather of the present clan chief. Sir Fitzroy was only a boy when he saw the ruined Duart Castle for the first time and reputedly uttered the words, 'It is going to be my life's ambition to restore the castle as a family home and headquarters of the clan.' This he achieved, with the aid of Scottish architect Sir John Burnet, at the age of seventy-six. Today, members of the Maclean Clan travel from all over the world to visit the ancestral home. Sir Fitzroy, a veteran of the Crimea, died a centenarian in 1936.

Earliest records suggest that the castle dates from the mid-13th century, since when the Clan Maclean have endured a colourful and sometimes bloody existence on Mull. The castle today contains much memorabilia, including some unusual horn snuffboxes and a horn container for wig powder dating from the early 18th century. The kitchen today is as it was in Sir Fitzroy Maclean's day and his new addition to the castle structure, the Sea Room, affords magnificent views of both the sea and the mountains. The banqueting hall, where the walls are nine feet thick in places, contains some family portraits and three regimental flags. The state room is furnished as it was for the honeymoon of Lord Maclean and his bride (parents of the present clan chief) during World War II.

One of Maclean's more infamous clansmen is one James Maclean (b.1724), 'The Gentleman Highwayman', whose story is told in a book on show at Duart. After squandering his fortune in 1748, James made a less than honourable attempt to amass another by means of highway robbery. This he did with great success.

Duart Castle on the Isle of Mull is the ancestral home of the Clan Maclean

DUNROBIN CASTLE Highland

½ mile (0.8km) north of Golspie | Open selected days April to October | Tel: 01408 633177 | **www.dunrobincastle.co.uk**

Like most ancient Scottish castles, Dunrobin started out as a keep, or tower, and is named after its originator, Earl Robin. It was built in the early 1300s and subsequent enlargements in the 17th, 18th and 19th centuries created the splendid, gleaming, turreted castle that today's visitors see. The original keep is still at its heart, and a tour of the castle as a whole gives a fascinating illustration of the development of architectural style over the centuries.

The overall impression of the state rooms, bedrooms and nurseries recalls the lifestyle of the Dukes of Sutherland in Victorian times. The furniture, pictures – including some Canalettos – family heirlooms and *objets d'art* have been carefully displayed in their original settings wherever possible, creating a true reflection of Dunrobin Castle as a family home and not simply as an historical exhibit.

There are a few surprises, though, notably when visitors step into the Sub Hall. Here, instead of the fine decor and furnishings one might expect to find is, as large as life, a 19th-century fire engine! Still in working order, it is hung with fire helmets and buckets, and watched over by the baleful stare of the collection of stags' heads on the wall.

Beyond the castle walls, in a converted summerhouse, a museum has been set out to display various collections that reflect the wide-ranging interests of the family over the centuries. These range from ornithology to Egyptology.

Equally as grand as the castle, the magnificent formal 19th-century gardens were modelled on those at Versailles. They were designed by Sir Charles Barry, who was the architect not only of Dunrobin's Victorian extension but also of the Houses of Parliament in London.

Dunrobin Castle, with its fairytale spires and turrets, is perched on a high terrace above walled gardens

DUNVEGAN CASTLE Isle of Skye

About 20 miles (32km) north west of Portree | Open daily April to October | Tel: 01470 521206 | **www.dunvegancastle.com**

This stronghold of the Clan MacLeod is still occupied by the Clan Chief – the 29th to be precise – who can trace a history back to the last Norse Kings of Man and the North Isles. The castle has been their home for nearly 800 years, and it is almost certain that it occupies the site of an earlier fort, which may predate it by 1,000 years.

Naturally enough, various additions have been made over the centuries, but the most substantial alterations were made by the 25th Chief, between 1840 and 1850. He commissioned Robert Brown of Edinburgh, at a cost of £8,000, to add dummy pepperpot towers and defensive battlements, and to undertake the rebuilding of the north wing.

Every room has its own story to tell. The drawing room is where you can see the famous Fairy Flag of Dunvegan, its fabric now protected by glass to prevent visitors from cutting off pieces to take home for good luck! The dining room forms the largest suite of rooms in the castle, with ancestral portraits covering over 300 years of family history. The library has a collection of books of historical and family interest, including the *Dunvegan Armorial*, compiled in 1582–84. Only a few feet away from the gracious surroundings of the drawing room is the dungeon, where prisoners were thrown, through a trap in the guardhouse floor, and left to die.

Dunvegan is linked with one of the most romantic stories of Scottish history. One of the illegitimate sons of the 22nd Chief married the daughter of Flora MacDonald (1722–90), who famously helped Bonnie Prince Charlie escape from government troops, dressed as her maidservant. Flora herself lived at Dunvegan for a time.

Picturesque Dunvegan Castle is the oldest continuously inhabited castle in Scotland

FALKLAND PALACE Fife

4½ miles (7km) north west of Glen Rothes | Open from March to October | Tel: 0844 493 2186 | **www.nts.org.uk**

The somewhat forbidding walls of Falkland Palace – likened by Scottish satirical writer Thomas Carlyle (1795–1881) to 'a black old bit of coffin or protrusive shin-bone sticking through the soil of the dead past' – encapsulate one of the most romantic periods of Scottish history. Within these walls you will find tales of political intrigue and murder, of hunting and hawking, of art and of literature.

This was the favourite home of the Stuart kings from the time of James II of Scotland until 1651, when Charles II abandoned theA palace to face his own defeat and exile. The fate of the palace at that time was equally dismal; it was occupied by Oliver Cromwell's troops, damaged by fire and allowed to fall into miserable ruin.

In 1887, though, the 3rd Marquess of Bute, a descendant of the Royal Stuarts, became Hereditary Keeper of the palace. He restored and rebuilt much of the palace and, though it is now in the care of the National Trust for Scotland, his descendant still lives in the building as Keeper.

Inside, Falkland Palace is furnished with huge old oak furniture, including an enormous four-poster bed said to have belonged to James VI, and rich wall hangings. The old library has a remarkable *trompe-l'oeil* ceiling and there are 17th-century Flemish 'Verdure' tapestries along the gallery leading to the King's apartments.

Falkland Palace also has a royal tennis court, which was built for James V in 1539 and therefore pre-dates Henry VIII's tennis court at Hampton Court Palace by more than eighty years.

An ornate lamp post stands in front of the somewhat forbidding twin towers of Falkland Palace's 16th-century gatehouse. The towers are adorned with the coat-of-arms of the Stuarts and of the 3rd Marquess of Bute, who restored the building in the 19th century

FLOORS CASTLE Roxburghshire

1 mile (1.5km) north west of Kelso | Open selected days throughout the year | Tel: 01573 223333 | **www.roxburghe.net**

The family home of the Innes Kers, Floors has been described as the largest inhabited mansion in Britain. It started its existence as a large house, built between 1718 and 1740 for the 1st Duke of Roxburghe, John Ker. Until recently it was believed that Sir John Vanbrugh had drawn up the plans, but it is now known to be the work of William Adam.

On the 1st Duke's death in 1740, the house quickly passed through his son Robert to John, the 3rd Duke, in 1755. The death of his heir, an elderly cousin, in the following year, sparked off a celebrated crisis – the Roxburghe Peerage Case – with a number of distant relatives eagerly claiming the title. The matter was finally decided in 1812 by the Committee of Privileges of the House of Lords, who came down in favour of Sir James

Innes. Taking the title 5th Duke and the name Innes Ker, Sir James was forced to sell his predecessor's famous library to cover the costs of his claim.

The 6th Duke, James, was to further the family fortunes through his connections at Court, earning himself a peerage, and a state visit from Queen Victoria in 1867 – a summerhouse in the garden was built especially for her. The 6th Duke was also responsible for changing the face of Floors, engaging the great Scottish architect William Playfair, noted for his work in Edinburgh New Town, to remodel and extend the house. Playfair added a delightful roofscape of lead cupolas more reminiscent of French than Scottish architectural traditions, as well as features ranging from the Grand Ballroom to

Floors Castle, with its spires and crenellations

a Gothic-style chamber to hold the Duke's collection of stuffed birds.

While the outside of Floors has barely changed since that time, extensive remodelling of the interior was undertaken during the time of the 8th Duke, Sir Henry Innes Ker, who inherited it in 1892. In 1903 the 8th Duke married American heiress, Mary Goelet. Her greatest contribution is probably the collection of antique tapestries, many brought from her Long Island home. Duchess May, as she was known, also acquired paintings by Matisse and ornaments by Fabergé. Together they form one of the chief attractions of Floors today.

GLAMIS CASTLE Angus

12 miles (19km) west of Dundee | Tel: 01307 840393 | www.glamis-castle.co.uk

Early records of Glamis show that it was a holy place where, in the 8th century, St Fergus came from Ireland to preach and to live out his life. Today, visitors can see St Fergus's Well near the kirk, and several Celtic stones found in the area date from that time. Later, Scottish royalty came to appreciate the lush Angus landscape and built a hunting lodge at Glamis. Shakespeare's witches were rather premature in naming Macbeth 'Thane of Cawdor and of Glamis', as the actual thaneage (or lordship) was not granted to

Glamis until 1264, a century after his death. The thaneage then became a feudal barony in 1376, when Sir John Lyon of Forteviot (Thane of Glamis) married King Robert II's daughter, Princess Joanna. And so began a line of feudal barons and, later, earls that continues to flourish at Glamis to this day.

The family became Bowes Lyon when the 9th Earl married a Durham heiress, Miss Mary Eleanor Bowes. The most famous Bowes Lyon was, of course, Her Majesty Queen Elizabeth, the Queen Mother (1900–2002).

The stunning exterior (above) and the chapel (left) at Glamis Castle, childhood home to the Queen Mother

When Lady Elizabeth Bowes Lyon married Prince Albert, the Duke of York, in 1923, her mother, Lady Strathmore, created a suite of rooms for the exclusive use of the royal couple. Although the Queen Mother was not born here, she spent most of her childhood at Glamis, and this is where she gave birth to her second daughter, Princess Margaret. The Royal Apartments are furnished with fine antiques and porcelain and family portraits, the most notable being one of the Queen Mother when she was Duchess of York.

The gardens at Glamis include a 5 acre (2ha) walled garden for vegetables, fruit and flowers and a delightful Dutch garden. On the east side of the castle is the Italian garden – about 2 acres (0.8ha) enclosed within a high yew hedge and featuring two 17th-century-style gazebos. This garden is entered through decorative wrought-iron gates, which were made to commemorate the eightieth birthday of the Queen Mother in 1980.

HOPETOUN HOUSE City of Edinburgh

1½ miles (2.5km) west of South Queensferry | Open daily Easter to end of September | Tel: 0131 331 2451 | **www.hopetoun.co.uk**

Hopetoun House is an amalgamation in style of two eminent Scottish architects. It was originally designed by Sir William Bruce for Charles Hope, 1st Earl of Hopetoun, and completed in 1707. Then, in 1721, the architect William Adam was commissioned to enlarge the house. After his death, work was continued by his sons, and the interior decoration was completed around 1767. Much of that original decoration in the main apartments still survives to this day. The two individual styles of architecture, both clearly discernible, are linked by the imposing entrance hall, which was redesigned in order to harmonize with Adam's alterations.

Pride of place, above the white marble fireplace in the entrance hall, is given to a massive portrait of the 7th Earl of Hopetoun, who became the first Governor-General of Australia and was created Marquess of Linlithgow. On the opposite wall is a portrait of his son, the 2nd Marquess, who was Britain's longest serving Viceroy of India (1936–43). Both are wearing the robes of Knight of the Thistle. They are great-grandfather and grandfather of the present Lord Linlithgow, the 4th Marquess. The Hope family is descended from one John Hope, a Burgess of Edinburgh, who died in 1561.

Entered from the hall, the state rooms were designed by William Adam and were decorated under the supervision of his son, John. The yellow silk damask on the walls in the Yellow Drawing Room is repeated on the sumptuous sofas, and the walls are lined with fine paintings and glittering gilt mirrors. A large number of interesting paintings adorn the walls of the Red Drawing Room, while an array of fine family portraits by such artists as Sir Henry Raeburn, Allan Ramsay and Gainsborough grace the walls of the State Dining Room.

The chief decorative feature of the William Bruce part of the house is the front stairs. Here, wood panelling with elaborate carving is enhanced by some decorative murals painted in 1967 by Scottish artist William McLaren.

The State Dining Room at Hopetoun House is hung with portraits of the great and good

INVERARAY CASTLE

Just north of Inveraray | Open daily April to October | Tel: 01499 302203 | www.inveraray-castle.com

The history of Clan Campbell dates back to 1266 and beyond, and could fill volumes, but the senior branch of the family, Earls of Argyll, moved into a fortified tower with a small settlement nearby, at the mouth of the River Aray, in the 15th century.

The dukedom was conferred on the 10th Earl by a grateful William of Orange in 1701; by 1720 the 2nd Duke, a great Hanoverian soldier, was thinking of remodelling the castle to designs by Sir John Vanbrugh – but it was his brother Archibald, succeeding him in 1743, who threw himself into the task.

Most of what can be seen at Inveraray today was planned by the 3rd Duke, including the township, the castle and the beautiful surrounding parkland. The foundation stone was laid in 1746, just yards away from the old tower (which was not demolished until 1773). The basic square structure, including the central tower, was completed by 1758 to a design by Roger Morris. One of the most appealing features of the estate was also built at this time: the watchtower high on Duniquaich was constructed in 1748, for £46.

There is a great sense of space and light in the State Dining Room, which was created from one end of the Long Gallery when a modest entrance hall was built in the middle in 1772. The elaborate wall paintings of flower garlands and fruit, with little animals, faces, peacock feathers and anything else that took the artist's fancy, are encased in finely gilded panels. With the central friezes, it is in the French style made popular by the young Prince of Wales at Carlton House, yet it is the only work to survive of the two French artists Girard and Guinard. The quality of the painting here and in the drawing room is unique and exquisite, enhanced by the pretty French tapestry work on the gilded furniture.

The Tapestry Drawing Room is hung with beautiful Beauvais tapestries, commissioned by the 5th Duke, with further painting on a delicate ceiling by Robert Adam. The floral themed room is dominated by a lovely portrait by Hoppner of the 5th Duke's daughter, Lady Charlotte, as 'Flora'.

**Below: A stunning aerial view of the castle
Right: The well-stocked Armoury Hall**

Before the architect John Kinross was called upon to improve Manderston, the old house, built in the late 18th century for Mr Dalhousie Weatherstone, was solid, square and unremarkable. In 1855, the estate was bought by William Miller who made his fortune in the trade of hemp and herrings. He went on to become Honorary British Consul at St Petersburg, then a Member of Parliament, which earned him a baronetcy in 1874.

Sir William intended, as is usual, to leave Manderston to his eldest son, also William, but he choked to death on a cherry stone at Eton in 1874, and the house passed to the second son, James. Sir James Miller was one of late Victorian England's most eligible bachelors and was accomplished as a sportsman, soldier and horseracing enthusiast. His sporting passion is reflected in the decor of the Ante-room where Diana, the goddess of hunting, is portrayed, and in the decoration of the ballroom and drawing room in primrose and white – Sir James's racing colours. James married Eveline Curzon, daughter of Lord Scarsdale, head of one of the most revered families in England. Sir James re-employed Kinross when he returned from the Boer War in 1901, instructing him to transform Manderston into a house that would resemble yet surpass Kedleston Hall, his bride's ancestral home in Derbyshire, in style and grandeur.

With the warmth and richness of Kedleston reproduced, Lady Eveline must truly have felt at home on entering the vestibule, with its gorgeous panels of apricot alabaster from Derbyshire, and the dining room has the largest private collection of Blue John in Scotland. This very rare, semi-precious stone is found nowhere else in the world but in Derbyshire. In the hall, the fireplace with its elaborate plasterwork is almost an exact copy of one at Kedleston.

Sir James and Lady Eveline held a ball at Manderston in 1905 to celebrate its completion. All too soon, sadly, their era was over, for in January 1906, just three months after completion, Sir James died.

Lady Eveline's feminine influence presides over many of the rooms. She also had a passion for fancy-dress soirées and loved to dress up as a Russian tsarina – perhaps influenced by the miscellaneous collection that her father-in-law brought back from St Petersburg.

The present Lord Palmer's great-grandmother embroidered the three Louis XVI chairs in front of the fireplace in the drawing room, and his grandmother worked on the corded silk of the four chairs opposite.

One of the fascinations of Manderston is that the life of the servants is also depicted. There are still bell-pulls in the bedrooms: 'up' called a maid whereas 'down' indicated the requirement of a manservant. Pity the poor servants before 1960, when the lift was installed – everything had to be carried upstairs, including coal.

The servants' hall in the basement is now the Racing Room. Sir James's horse, Sainfoin, won the Derby in 1890 at 25-1, and he won £118,000 over a sixteen-year period. The kitchen at Manderston has four ovens for varying temperatures. A jug of beer would always be available to departing tradesmen.

Left: Manderston House and Garden
Right: The Great Hall with its inlaid marble floor

MELLERSTAIN HOUSE Border

7 miles (11km) north west of Kelso | Open selected days Easter to October | Tel: 01573 410225/410636 | **www.mellerstain.com**

The estate at Mellerstain had changed hands several times before it was made over, in 1643, to one George Baillie of Jerviswood by Charles II. Of the house already on the site, called Whiteside (or Whytesyde), little is known and nothing remains today.

George's son Robert, a staunch supporter of the rebellious Duke of Monmouth, was condemned to death for high treason in 1684; the estate was forfeited until after 1688, when Robert's son George returned from exile in Holland in the retinue of the Prince of Orange, soon to be King William II.

This George Baillie, whose portrait by Sir John Medina may be seen in the Small Sitting Room, was married to the redoutable Lady Grisell Baillie, daughter of another loyal Covenanter. George rose to be a Lord of the Treasury (many books in the library bear his special bookplate, dated 1724), and in 1725 he laid the foundations of the new mansion at Mellerstain. Designed by the architect William Adam, who created the two symmetrical wings, the building was completed by Adam's son, Robert. The gardens were laid out with a distant lake in the form of a Dutch canal – a reminder, perhaps, of the Baillies' exile.

The Baillies' younger daughter Rachel married Charles, Lord Binning, heir to the earldom of Haddington; their elder son Thomas inherited the title to become the 7th Earl, while their younger son George Hamilton inherited Mellerstain and changed his name to Baillie. A charming portrait of him by Ramsay hangs in the music room, near one of his wife, by Gainsborough. George employed Robert Adam to complete the house, and its interior represents some of Adam's finest work. It is beautifully proportioned, and ceilings, fireplaces, mirrors and door furnishings have remained intact. The library is outstanding, its ceiling (c. 1773) painted in the original soft colours reminiscent of Wedgwood china.

Mellerstain was designed by William Adam and completed by his more famous son, Robert

PAXTON HOUSE Border

5 miles (8km) west of Berwick-upon-Tweed | Open daily from April to October for guided tours | Tel: 01289 386291 | **www.paxtonhouse.co.uk**

Paxton House's Picture Gallery was built in the Regency style, with elegant curved walls

Overlooking the River Tweed to the south, Paxton House numbers among its many attractions the largest private art gallery in Scotland, which is now an out-station of the National Galleries of Scotland. Furnished with fine rosewood pieces by William Trotter, the celebrated cabinet maker, the gallery was designed in 1811 by the architect, Robert Reid, who played an inspired part in designing Edinburgh's New Town – a grand scheme of well-proportioned Georgian terraces, crescents and squares.

The house itself was built in 1758 for Patrick Home of Billie, later the 13th Laird of Wedderburn. His intention was to create a fine home for himself and his prospective bride, one Miss Sophie de Brandt, a lady-in-waiting at the court of Frederick the Great – whose natural daughter she was suspected to be. Home had met her at Charlottenburg Palace near Berlin and had fallen instantly in love, but the marriage was not to be, and his only reminder of his loved one was a pair of kid gloves she had given him; these are still on display in the house.

Paxton House is one of the best examples of Palladian architecture in Britain, of which there are many. It was the work of the celebrated Adam brothers, and Robert Adam later added decorative plasterwork to the main public rooms. The impressive mahogany furniture in the entrance hall, dining room, breakfast parlour and main bedrooms came from Thomas Chippendale, and all the pieces have stood the test of time with quiet pride.

Eighty acres (32ha) of gardens and grounds surround the house and include lovely riverside walks and a children's adventure playground.

SCONE PALACE Perth & Kinross

3 miles (5km) north of Perth | Open daily April to end of October | Tel: 01738 552300 | **www.scone-palace.co.uk**

Since the 9th century the site of Scone Palace has occupied a place in history for the coronations of Scottish kings. Early records tell of a monastery here and then an Abbey of Augustinian Canons, but the Abbey and the Bishop's House were burned down in 1559 by a mob incited by the sermons of John Knox. Fortunately, the Palace of Scone, residence of the Abbot and coronation place of kings, survived. It was around this early structure that the present palace grew, enlarged in 1802, in a Gothic style in keeping with its monastic past, by the architect William Atkinson. The palace was then under the ownership of David William Murray, 3rd Earl cf Mansfield. He was the first Earl of Mansfield to have lived at Scone – the previous two considered life at Scone to be too austere, preferring to live in their comfortable southern estates. So the Murray family have the 3rd Earl to thank for the magnificent structure that exists today.

The Gothic inf uence in design is nowhere more enchanting than in the pretty Ante-room, painted in white with architectural details highlighted in gold and silver. There is a Chinese theme to this room, with its niches filled with vases from the Chien Lung period (1736–95) and some Chinese Chippendale chairs. The Gothic style continues in the majestic Long Gallery, some 142 feet (43m) long, with an unusual floor of Scottish oak inset with bog oak. Family portraits line the walls, and the gallery also contains Lord Mansfield's unique collection of Vernis Martin ware – papier-mâché made by the Martin family in 18th-century France. The library is home to a fabulous collection of 18th- and 19th-century porcelain.

An opulent room from Queen Victoria's suite. The Queen particularly requested ground-floor apartments

This fairytale castle has been the home of the Maitland family, Earls of Lauderdale, since the 13th century. The Maitlands came to Britain with William the Conqueror and headed north. Over the centuries the family became powerful through military and public service. One William Maitland was Secretary to Mary, Queen of Scots; his brother John was Lord Chancellor of Scotland in the mid-16th century and his grandson, also John, became one of the most important and controversial figures of 17th-century Scotland. Chief Scottish adviser and confidant of Charles II, he was made Secretary of State for Scotland at the Restoration and wielded unrivalled power and influence. On his marriage to the Countess of Dysart, John Maitland was created Duke of Lauderdale and this prompted his remodelling of Thirlestane Castle into a suitably grand residence.

Sir William Bruce was the architect who created a splendid palace without destroying the character of the original castle. He also supervised the interior work, which included some magnificent plasterwork in the state rooms. The Duke died in 1682 and, with no male heir, his title died with him. His brother, Charles, became the 3rd Earl of Lauderdale.

Visitors may well complete a tour of the castle with a crick in their neck from gazing up at all the wonderful ceilings – the richest of all is in the Large Drawing Room – but in every room it is worth looking upwards. Fine 19th-century French Empire-style furniture, vast gilded mirrors and one of the most comprehensive collections of family portraits in Scotland adorn the state rooms. The charming nurseries house a delightful collection of historic toys, with some modern replicas, too, for visiting children to play with, as well as a dressing-up chest.

Amazing ceilings are a feature of Thirlestane Castle. This one is in the Duke's Bedroom

TRAQUAIR HOUSE

Border

6 miles (10km) south east of Peebles | Open daily April to end of October; weekends only in November | Tel: 01896 830323 | www.traquair.co.uk

The ancient house of Traquair was once called a castle, but it has never withstood a siege or been fought over in bloody battle. Its exterior is remarkably plain, its high walls regularly punctuated with unornamented windows that break into the line of the high, steeply pitched roof. A hint of a turret in the centre marks one corner of the oldest section, but otherwise Traquair is refreshingly free of crenellations, castellations, machicolations, Gothic windows and all the other architectural paraphernalia without which no 18th-century stately home was considered complete. Yet, by its bulk and its bearing, and its romantic setting in the forest, it is every inch a castle. Visitors who flock to this Borders beauty spot will find that the fundamental honesty of Traquair is continued inside. With the exception, perhaps, of the library, there is little sign of lavish Georgian refurbishment or opulent Victorian High Gothic pastiche, and little to show in the way of unnecessary trinkets, for the family's fortune was spent in other,

arguably more noble causes. To some Traquair is a monument to lost causes, the visible sign of a family that simply fought too often on the wrong side; to others, it is a quiet, living, breathing home, minding its own business and continuing much as it has done for hundreds of years.

According to tradition – and tradition plays an important part at Traquair – the first building on this prime site, in a bend of the Tweed and the Quair burn, was probably a simple hut, used as a base for hunting in the surroundings of Ettrick Forest. This early reference dates the spot to about the year 950, but Traquair was first recognized as a royal hunting lodge in 1107 by King Alexander I of Scotland, who stayed here and granted its charter. Traquair remained a royal property until the 13th century and, though it was essentially little more than a fortified house, it was known at this time as Traquair Castle.

Lady Louisa Stuart became 15th Lady of Traquair in 1861. She was also unmarried, and lived on alone in the house into her

100th year – her photograph may be seen in the Still Room. On her death in 1875 she left money for the building of Catholic churches in Peebles and Innerleithen, and Traquair passed to her cousin, Henry Constable Maxwell of Terregles, who took the additional surname of Stuart.

He was intrigued by gemstones from around the world and amassed a fine collection in a small room at the top of the house. Unfortunately the collection was sold off on his death by his sons, who had no idea of their real value. The 17th and 18th Lairds, Herbert and Arthur, were conservative bachelors, determined to change nothing in the house. Through their nephew it passed eventually to the care of Peter Constable Maxwell Stuart, who became the 20th Laird. He and his wife, Flora, were responsible for much of the careful restoration work at Traquair, as well as the study of the family's history, and this work is continued by their daughter Catherine, who was brought up in this lovely old house and became 21st Lady of Traquair in 1990.

Inside Traquair's plain white exterior there are countless beautiful rooms stuffed with treasures

INDEX

A

Abbotsford, Melrose 193, 194
Adam, John 149, 195, 211
Adam, Robert 43, 49, 77, 92, 125–6, 149, 154, 164, 177, 201, 212, 216, 217
Adam, William 195, 201, 211, 216
Adlington Hall, Cheshire 147, 148
Albert, Prince Consort 74, 106
Alexander I, King of Scotland 220
Alfred the Great, King 45
Allanson, Robert 33
Alnwick Castle, Northumberland 149
Althorp, Northamptonshire 98
Anne, Queen 17, 51, 52
Anne of Cleves 66
Anne of Denmark 53
Arbury Hall, Warwickshire 99
Argyll, Earls of 212
Arley Hall, Cheshire 150
Armstrong, 1st Lord 151, 159
Arniston House, Midlothian 195
Arundel Castle, West Sussex 49, 50
Astor, William Waldorf 66
Athelhampton, Dorset 11, 12
Atholl, Earls of 199
Atkinson, William 56, 194, 218
Ayton Castle, Border 196–7

B

Ballindalloch Castle, Moray 198
Bamburgh Castle, Northumberland 151
Barry, Sir Charles 67, 206
Bath, Marquesses of 6, 30
Beauchamp family 144
Beaulieu, Hampshire 78
Bedford, Dukes of 49
Berkeley Castle, Gloucestershire 11, 13
Bess of Hardwick 104, 118
The Bishop's Palace, Wells, Somerset 14–15
Blair Castle, P & K 193, 199
Blathwayt, William 23
Blenheim Palace, Oxfordshire 49, 51
Blomfield, Sir Arthur 78
Blomfield, Sir Reginald 88
Bodryddan Hall, Denbighshire 97, 100
Boleyn, Anne 42, 49, 66, 84
Bower, Denys Eyre 56
Bowhill, Border 193, 200
Braemar Castle, Aberdeenshire 201
Breamore House, Hampshire 52
Brettingham, Matthew 112, 125
Broughton Castle, Oxfordshire 53

Brown, 'Capability' 19, 39, 43, 92, 101, 144, 148, 149, 164, 188, 195
Bruce, Sir William 211, 219
Bulwer-Lytton, Edward 70
Burges, William 27
Burghley House, Lincolnshire 97, 101
Burton Agnes Hall, Yorkshire 152–3
Burton Constable Hall, East Yorkshire 154

C

Cadhay, Devon 16
Caerhaes, Cornwall 8
Calke Abbey, Derbyshire 102
Campbell, Colen 123, 157
Capesthorne Hall, Cheshire 155
Carr of York, John 154, 164, 177, 180, 181, 188
Carriera, Rosalba 36
Castle Howard, Yorkshire 147, 156
Catherine of Aragon 65
Cawdor Castle, Highland 202
Cecil, William 101
Chambers, Sir William 60, 164
Charlecote Park, Warwickshire 103
Charles, Prince of Wales 98
Charles I, King 20, 28, 42, 52, 62, 143, 170
Charles II, King 43, 52, 58, 60, 83, 208, 216
Charlie, Bonnie Prince 204, 207
Chartwell, Kent 54
Chatsworth, Derbyshire 104–5
Chavenage House, Gloucestershire 17
Chenies Manor House, Hertfordshire 49, 55
Chiddingstone Castle, Kent 49, 56
Chillingham Castle, Northumberland 157
Chipchase Castle, Northumberland 158
Churchill, Sir Winston 51, 54, 70
Chute family 93
Clandon Park, Surrey 57
Clevedon Court, Somerset 18
Clifford family 43
Coke, Thomas 122
Conwy, Sir John 100
Cooke, Sir Robert 12
Corsham Court, Wiltshire 19
Cotehele, Cornwall 20–1
Cotton family 44
Courtenay family 34
Crace, John 27, 70
Cragside, Northumberland 159

Cromwell, Oliver 17, 22, 38, 73, 106, 208
Cubitt, Thomas 74
Curzon, Lord 125–6

D

Dalemain, Cumbria 160
Dalmeny House, Edinburgh 203
Dashwood, Sir Francis 94, 116
Deene Park, Northamptonshire 106
Denham, Sir John 44
Dent family 42
Devonshire, Dukes of 104–5, 167–8
Diana, Princess of Wales 49, 68, 98
Digby family 39
Doddington Hall, Lincolnshire 107
Dorfold Hall, Cheshire 161
Dorney Court, Berkshire 49, 58
Douglas family 204
Drumlanrig Castle, Dumfries & Galloway 193, 204
Duart Castle, Isle of Mull 205
Dunrobin Castle, Highland 193, 206
Dunster Castle, Somerset 8, 22
Dunvegan Castle, Isle of Skye 193, 207
Dyrham Park, Gloucestershire 23

E

Eastnor Castle, Herefordshire 97, 108
Edward, Black Prince 120
Edward I, King 157, 169
Edward II, King 11, 13
Edward IV, King 151
Edward VI, King 80
Edward VII, King 60, 81
Egerton-Warburton, Rowland 150
Eliot, George 99
Elizabeth I, Queen 19, 30, 39, 42, 44, 55, 59, 66, 71, 79, 83
Elizabeth, the Queen Mother 81, 189, 210
Elton, Sir Edmund 18
Elton Hall, Cambridgeshire 109
Erddig, Wrexham 110–11
Euston Hall, Norfolk 112
Eyam Hall, Derbyshire 113
Eyre family 32

F

Fairfax House, Yorkshire 162
Falkland Palace, Fife 208
Fiennes family 53
Firle Place, East Sussex 59
Fitzalan family 50
Floors Castle, Border 209

Forde Abbey, Somerset 7, 24
Fursdon, Devon 25

G

Gage family 59
Gawsworth Hall, Cheshire 163
George I, King 52, 68
George II, King 52, 68
Gibbons, Grinling 69, 101, 204
Gibbs, James 69, 123, 138
Glamis Castle, Angus 193, 210
Goodwood House, West Sussex 49, 60
Gorges, Sir Edward 32
Grafton, Dukes of 112
Great Dixter, East Sussex 61
Greville, Mrs 81
Grey, Lady Jane 42, 59, 92
Grey family 157
Grimsthorpe Castle, Lincolnshire 114

H

Haddon Hall, Derbyshire 115
Hagley Hall, West Midlands 116
Ham House, London 62–3
Hammerwood Park, West Sussex 64
Hampton Court, London 65
Hansom, Joseph 129
Hardwick Hall, Derbyshire 117–18
Hardy, Thomas 12
Harewood House, West Yorkshire 147, 164–5
Harpur family 102
Harris, Thomas 141
Hartland Abbey, Devon 6, 26
Haydon family 16
Heathcoat-Amory, John 27
Hedingham Castle, Essex 119
Hellen's, Herefordshire 97, 120–1
Henry II, King 13
Henry III, King 127, 157
Henry VI, King 176
Henry VII, King 44
Henry VIII, King 7, 26, 28, 42, 49, 55, 65, 66, 71, 80, 109, 139
Heron family 158
Hertford, Marquesses of 138
Hever Castle, Kent 49, 66
Highclere Castle, Berkshire 49, 67
Hoghton Tower, Lancashire 166
Holker Hall, Cumbria 167–8
Holkham Hall, Norfolk 97, 122
Hopetoun House, Edinburgh 193, 211
Hopper, Thomas 130, 132, 134
Houghton Hall, Norfolk 97, 123
Howard, Catherine 59

Howard family 50
Hulse, Edward 52
Hutton-in-the-Forest, Cumbria 169
Huyshe family 38

I
Ingatestone Hall, Essex 124
Ingilby family 181
Inverary Castle, Argyllshire 193, 212–13

J
James I, King 39, 71, 166, 170, 179, 181, 201
John, King 13
Jones, Inigo 45

K
Keck, Anthony 130
Kedleston Hall, Derbyshire 125–6
Kensington Palace, London 49, 68
Kent, William 68, 123
Kentwell Hall, Suffolk 97, 127
Kingston Bagpuize House, Oxfordshire 69
Kinross, John 215
Kiplin Hall, North Yorkshire 170
Knebworth House, Hertfordshire 49, 70
Knightshayes Court, Devon 27

L
Lacock Abbey, Wiltshire 8, 28
Lanhydrock House, Cornwall 29
Lascelles family 164
Latrobe, Benjamin 64
Lauderdale, Duchess of 62
Layer Marney Tower, Essex 128
Legh family 147, 148
Leighton Hall, Lancashire 147, 171
Leoni, Giacomo 57
Levens Hall, Cumbria 147, 172–3
Little Malvern Court, Worcestershire 129
Lloyd, Christopher 61
Longleat, Wiltshire 6, 11, 30
Loseley House, Surrey 71
Lucy family 103
Luttrell family 8, 22, 26
Lutyens, Sir Edwin 61, 70
Lyttelton family 116

M
MacKenzie, Thomas 198
Maclean, Sir Fitzroy 205
Maitland family 219
Manderston, Border 193, 214–15
Margham Country Park, Neath 130
Marlborough, Dukes of 49, 51
Mary, Queen of Scots 104, 118, 180, 204

Mary I, Queen 65
Melbourne Hall, Derbyshire 131
Mellerstain House, Border 216
Meols Hall, Lancashire 174
Methuen family 19
Michelham Priory, East Sussex 72
Mirehouse, Cumbria 175
Molesworth-St Aubyn family 33
Montacute House, Somerset 31
More family 71
Morgan family 143
Morris, William 86, 163
Muncaster Castle, Cumbria 147, 176
Munthe, Hilda 84, 120
Murray, William 62

N
Nash, John 19
Nelson, Lord 32
Nether Winchendon House, Buckinghamshire 73
Newby Hall, Yorkshire 147, 177
Newhouse, Wiltshire 32
Norfolk, Dukes of 49, 50
Northumberland, Dukes of 49, 92

O
Opie, John 36
Osborne House, Isle of Wight 9, 74–5
Osterley, Middlesex 76–7

P
Paine, James 125, 189
Palace House, Beaulieu, Hampshire 78
Palmer family 58
Parham Park, West Sussex 79
Parr, Katherine 42
Paxton House, Border 217
Pencarrow House, Cornwall 33
Penrhyn Castle, Gwynedd 8, 132–4
Penshurst Place, Kent 80
Peover Hall, Cheshire 178
Percy family 149, 157
Petre family 124
Phelips, Sir Edward 31
Pinnegar, David 64
Plas Mawr, Conwy 135
Plas Newydd, Gwynedd 136
Plas yn Rhiw, Gwynedd 137
Playfair, William 209
Polesden Lacey, Surrey 81
Powderham Castle, Devon 11, 34–5
Powell-Cotton, Major Percy 82
Preston Tower, Northumberland 179
Prideaux, Edmund 24
Prideaux family 36
Prideaux Place, Cornwall 36
Pugin, Augustus 108

Q
Quex Park, Kent 49, 82

R
Raby Castle, County Durham 147, 180
Ragley Hall, Warwickshire 138
Raleigh, Sir Walter 39
Raphael, Marlie 69
Reid, Robert 217
Richard III, King 144
Richmond, Dukes of 49, 60
Ripley Castle, Yorkshire 181
Robartes, Lord 29
Robinson, Sir Thomas 183
Rockingham Castle, Leicestershire 139
Rode Hall, Cheshire 182
Rokeby Park, County Durham 183
Rosebery, Earls of 203
Roxburghe, Dukes of 209
Rutland, 9th Duke of 115
Rydal Mount, Cumbria 147, 184

S
Sackville family 72
St Aubyn family 37
St Mary's House, West Sussex 83
St Michael's Mount, Cornwall 37
Salvin, Anthony 150, 155, 169, 176
Sand, Devon 38
Sandys family 93
Scone Palace, P & K 193, 218
Scott, Sir George Gilbert 42
Scott, Sir Walter 157, 193, 194, 200
Seaton Delaval Hall, Northumberland 185
Shakespeare, William 46, 103, 166, 210
Sherborne Castle, Dorset 39
Shipton Hall, Shropshire 140
Sidney family 80
Sizergh Castle, Cumbria 186–7
Sledmere House, Yorkshire 147, 188
Smirke, Robert 108
Smithson, Robert 152
Smythson, Robert 30, 107, 118
Southside House, London 84
Spencer family 98
Squerryes Court, Kent 85
Standen, West Sussex 86–7
Stansted Park, West Sussex 6, 88
Stanway House, Gloucestershire 40–1
Stockeld Park, Yorkshire 189
Stokesay Court, Shropshire 141
Stonor Park, Oxfordshire 89

Stowe House and Gardens, Buckinghamshire 90–1
Streatfeild family 56
Stucley family 26
Sudeley Castle, Gloucestershire 11, 42
Sykes family 188
Syon House, Middlesex 49, 92

T
Talbot, William Henry Fox 28
Talman, William 23, 88
Temple family 90
Teulon, SS 64
Thirlestane Castle, Border 219
Thynne, John 30
Tracy family 40
Traquair House, Border 193, 220–1
Tredegar House, Newport 97, 142–3

U
Ugbrooke Park, Devon 43

V
Vanbrugh, Sir John 51, 113, 156, 185, 209, 212
Victoria, Queen 68, 74, 95, 106, 129, 134, 156, 209
The Vine, Basingstoke 49, 93

W
Wallington, Northumberland 190–1
Walpole, Sir Robert 123
Walwyn, Fulke 120
Warwick Castle, Warwickshire 97, 144
Webb, Philip 86
Wellington, Duke of 52, 60, 172
West Wycombe Park, Buckinghamshire 94
Weston Park, Shropshire 97, 145
Whittington Court, Gloucestershire 44
Wightwick, George 33
Wilbraham family 182
Wilkins, William 203
William III, King 23, 65, 68, 104
William the Conqueror 139, 149, 151
Wilton House, Wiltshire 11, 45–7
Woburn Abbey, Bedfordshire 49, 95
Wolfe, General 85
Wolsey, Cardinal 65
Wordsworth, William 184
Wren, Sir Christopher 65, 68, 69, 99
Wriothesley, Sir Thomas 78
Wyatt, James 34, 45, 60, 88, 136, 138, 154
Wyatville (Wyatt), Jeffrey 157, 203
Wynn, Robert 135

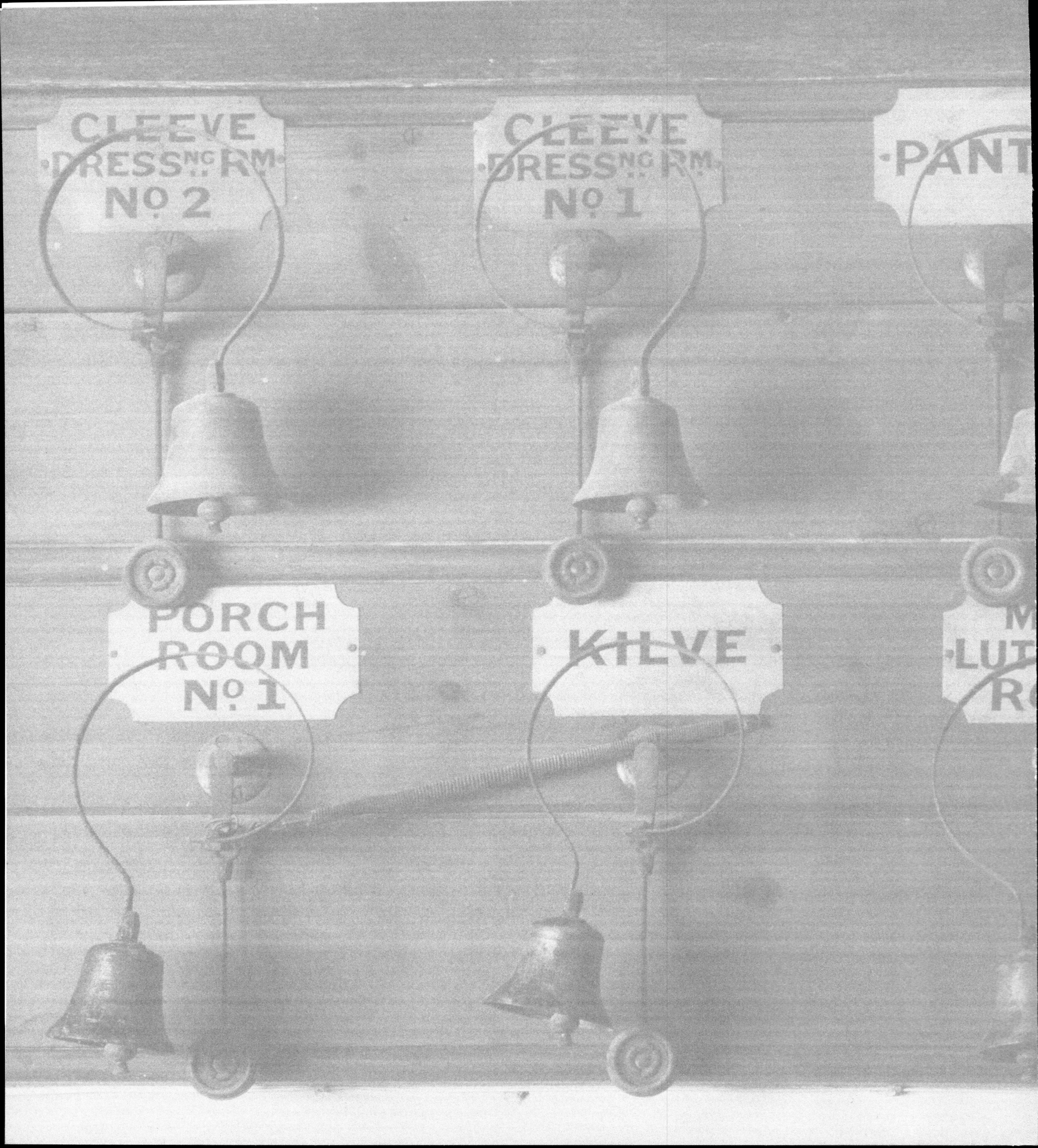

CLEEVE DRESSNG RM No 2
CLEEVE DRESSNG RM No 1
PORCH ROOM No 1
KILVE